THE ADVANCED GUIDE TO
RADIO CONTROL
SPORT FLYING

THE ADVANCED GUIDE TO
RADIO CONTROL
SPORT FLYING

DOUGLAS R. PRATT

TAB BOOKS Inc.
Blue Ridge Summit, PA

FIRST EDITION
FIRST PRINTING

Copyright © 1988 by TAB BOOKS Inc.
Printed in the United States of America

Library of Congress Cataloging in Publication Data

Pratt, Douglas R.
The advanced guide to radio control sport flying.

Includes index.
1. Airplanes—Models—Radio Control.   I. Title.
TL770.P67   1988   629.133′134   88-2267
ISBN 0-8306-9360-2 (pbk.)

Questions regarding the content of this book
should be addressed to:

Reader Inquiry Branch
TAB BOOKS Inc.
Blue Ridge Summit, PA 17294-0214

Contents

Introduction

THIS BOOK IS THE COMPANION VOLUME TO *THE Beginner's Guide to Radio Control Sport Flying* (TAB Book #3020). I wrote these two books for the average, noncompetitive RC flier. Most RC fliers are sport fliers, who are in this hobby for their own pleasure rather than to win trophies. My idea was to put information in these two books that sport fliers need to continue enjoying their hobby.

These books have many descriptions of specific products: kits, engines, radios, accessories. I believe that people want to read about things that they're thinking of buying or that they've just bought. I know that some of these products may not be available by the time you read this, but it shouldn't matter. You can apply the descriptions to many similar products that you might be using.

Appendix A at the back of the book contains a list of hobby manufacturers. This list doesn't cover every company in the industry, of course, but most of the important ones are there. Please note that you can almost always purchase these companies' products at your local hobby shop. If your dealer hasn't got the item in stock, he can get it. Manufac-

turer addresses are included here so you can write to them for current catalogs and product information. If you're not lucky enough to have a hobby store near you, there are reputable mail-order firms listed in the same index.

RC Frequencies

Since the FCC approved new space for RC frequencies, the AMA has set regulations for gradually phasing them in. You need to understand how this system works, so that you know what frequencies are proper to use. You'll find a complete discussion of RC frequencies in *The Beginner's Guide to Radio Control Sport Flying*. Meanwhile, you can always get the latest, most accurate information by writing to the AMA's Technical Director, Bob Underwood. The address is in the Appendices.

AMA

The Academy of Model Aeronautics is the nationwide organization of model fliers. AMA has been in existence for over 50 years, and they have been crucial in the development of RC flying. If it wasn't for AMA, we'd all have to pass a test (including Morse code), pay a fee, and get a Ham Radio license to operate RC equipment. AMA's close work with the FCC has given us the present frequency situation, where we will have 50 frequencies to use license-free in 1991. AMA also maintains the world's largest model airplane museum in their headquarters building near Washington, DC. They publish *Model Aviation* magazine as a service to their members. They host the annual National Model Airplane Championships. And they do much more. Any serious RC flier should be an AMA member.

Chances are that your flying club will require that you belong to AMA before you can use their flying field. There's a very important reason for this: Joining AMA gives you a substantial amount of insurance coverage while you are building and flying your models. If your model goes out of control and causes an accident, your AMA insurance will cover it. If you should hurt yourself while building or flying, and your own medical insurance won't cover it, your AMA insurance will. There's even coverage for fire, theft, or vandalism of your model equipment. The AMA Chartered model flying clubs have AMA liability insurance protection. Chartered clubs can even extend the liability coverage to the owner of their flying field. In this lawsuit-happy age, AMA insurance has made it possible to use thousands of flying fields that would be closed without it.

Any way you look at it, AMA membership is a bargain. If you're not an AMA member, ask your hobby shop for an application form, or contact AMA Headquarters for more information; the address is in the Appendices.

Chapter 1

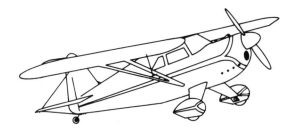

Electric Power

ELECTRIC POWER FOR MODEL AIRPLANES IS JUST beginning to hit in a big way. There has been a lot of progress in the art, and there is a good array of products available for the electric flier. But it's been a long, hard road to get to this point, with many disappointments along the way.

Several years ago, electric model kits were released that were inferior products. They were marginally successful at best, and really only performed well in the hands of a skilled pilot. So electric power got a bad reputation, because people bought things with unrealistic expectations. I still hear people grudgingly admit that electric power is all right for some lighter planes or Old-Timers, but it really doesn't work well for anything else.

It's a bum rap. Electric power is here to stay. It has lots of advantages over gas: It's cleaner, quieter, and more convenient. True, the power-to-weight ratio of an electric power system is less favorable than a gas model's powerplant. This means that an electric motor and its battery will produce less usable power than a gas engine and tank of fuel weighing the same. But the performance gap is nar-

rowing all the time, thanks to new motor technology, new battery design, and new building techniques. Meanwhile, the products available today are quite adequate to fly just about anything you care to fly—and do it well.

ELECTRIC MODEL DIFFERENCES

Electric models are different. You need to be aware of certain things before venturing into electric models. First of all, they *are* less powerful than gas models. This means that they generally require larger wings and will not fly as fast as a similar gas-powered plane. But unless your main interest is racing, you won't mind the lower flying speed; it's usually a big help.

Electric models carry most of their weight in the battery pack. The weight of the batteries is always a significant fraction of the total weight of the aircraft—sometimes more than 50 percent. So an electric plane should carry its batteries close to the center of gravity. They should also be carried low, so in the event of a crash or a hard landing, the bat-

1

teries won't destroy much of the structure. I find it most convenient to have the battery pack accessible through a hatch in the bottom of the plane. As an added bonus, you don't have to take off the wing to change battery packs.

Propeller selection is crucial with electric motors, and minor variations that wouldn't make a difference on a gas job can be vastly different on electrics. Start out with the prop recommended by the engine manufacturer; most often, this will be the prop to stick with. But when you start to experiment, do it gradually—an inch of diameter or pitch at a time.

ELECTRIC SAFETY

There are a couple of special safety factors to consider with electric airplanes. The batteries store a *lot* of energy—more than enough to tear themselves apart if it's all released at once. Shorting a battery pack could cause a fire.

Never take a pair of diagonal wire cutters and clip both wires from a battery pack at once! This will cause a direct short through the metal cutter blades. The insulation will burn off the wires almost instantly, so you won't be able to separate them. I learned this one the hard way, and it made quite an impression on me!

If you accidentally stick your finger into the prop of a running gas engine, the engine stops running. Not so with an electric motor! If you've gotten a cut from the prop, your attention will be diverted to your injury and the plane could get out of your control. So treat running electric motors with even more respect than you give to gas engines.

When a gas-powered model crashes, the motor stops running. Once again, the electric motor doesn't! The battery is putting all its power into trying to turn the prop. If the model is on its nose and the prop can't turn, all that power turns to heat. The result is a ruined motor and a burned-out battery pack. *Always* use a fuse, or a switch that allows you to turn the motor off from the transmitter, or *both*—preferably both, since the switch won't protect the power system if you lose control for some reason.

COBALT OR NOT COBALT?

Electric motors with samarium cobalt magnets can cost half again as much as motors with ferrite magnets, or more. Are they worth it?

As is so often the case, it depends on the airplane. A light airplane with plenty of wing will fly just fine with a standard ferrite motor. Some planes will make very good use of the cheap motors being sold for RC cars; in fact, there are several kits that tell you to use car motors.

Cobalt motors are considerably more powerful than ferrite motors, but they will drain the batteries faster. So if you are converting a gas-powered airplane to electric, consider a cobalt motor. A plane that will get to altitude quickly, then soar with power

The advent of motors with cobalt magnets gave electric fliers more power to work with. Right to left: Astro 05, 10, 15 and 40 Cobalt motors. (Photo courtesy Astro Flight)

The Astro 05 Cobalt mounted easily on the Geier's motor platform. I used the bolts that hold the metal gearbox in place to attach the motor to the metal motor mount. (Photo by Jennifer Pratt)

off, is a good candidate for a cobalt motor and a lightweight battery pack. Any application where you want speed rather than duration calls for a cobalt motor.

GEAR DRIVES

A gear drive unit serves the purpose of reducing the speed delivered to the propeller. This increases the torque, so you can swing a bigger, deeper-pitched prop than you would be able to put on the motor shaft. Is this better? Again, it all depends on the plane. Direct drive is better for more speed; just as with gas engines, you get higher speed from smaller props turning at higher rpm. So for a small, sport airplane with a relatively small wing, direct drive will be fine. But gearing a motor will be a real benefit to a plane with plenty of wing, designed to fly more slowly but stay up longer. Old-Timers, sailplanes, and scale models of slow-flying airplanes like Piper Cubs will all require gear drives.

There are several different gear drive units available. Astro Flight sells a gear drive for every motor they make, and they make the widest assortment of motors available to the hobby market. Leisure Electronics makes an excellent prop drive unit for their LT50 motor, the standard power package for many popular Old-Timer designs. Several Robbe engines come fitted with gear drives to handle their big banana-shaped two- and three-blade folding props. Graupner gear drives are imported by Hobby Lobby and available in hobby stores or by mail order.

I've recently gotten a look at a unique prop drive unit sold by Davey Systems.

BATTERY SELECTION

The choice of battery pack for your engine will depend on the engine, the airplane, and the kind of performance you want from the plane. The size of the cells determines the current available to the motor (in amps). The number of cells you use in the battery pack determines the voltage of the pack.

800 or 1200 mAh Cells?

Ni-cad batteries are rated in terms of the current they are capable of delivering. This is expressed in ampere-hours (Ah), or more commonly, milliamp-hours (mAh). If a battery pack is rated at 1200 mAh, it can provide 1200 milliamps (mA) for an hour, or 2400 mA for half an hour, etc.

The batteries we usually use to power our receivers have 500 mAh cells. Since receivers and servos usually require about 100 to 200 mA as they operate, a 500 mAh battery pack can power the airborne radio system for more than a couple of hours. Some smaller electric power systems will use 500 mAh cells, but the most common cells used for motors are 800 or 1200 mAh.

Eight-hundred mAh cells are slightly larger than 500 mAh cells, which are the size of the familiar AA "penlight" batteries. Twelve-hundred mAh cells are slightly smaller than standard C cells, and are often referred to as "sub-C" cells. These designations refer to the size and weight of each battery, not to its electrical capacity.

Twelve-hundred mAh cells are what you always find in RC cars, and they have been the standard in electric airplanes for many years. Sub-C cells are very powerful, and will handle a high charge current so they can recharge quickly. But their weight has always been a problem.

When 800 mAh cells came along a few years ago, they made an immediate hit. They're light, compact, and easy to work with. They don't have the power of the sub-C cells, but they have a slightly higher power density, meaning that for their weight they carry slightly more power than sub-c cells. And because they're smaller, a seven-cell pack of 800 mAh cells weighs about the same as a six-cell pack of sub-C cells! Motors that like higher voltages will be happy with 800 mAh cells in the system.

I've gradually converted almost all of my electric airplanes to 800 mAh packs over the last year or so. In several planes, such as my Leisure Senior Playboy, it's hard to tell the difference between a six-cell 1200 mAh pack and a seven-cell 800 mAh

pack; they both provide consistent flights of eight to nine minutes. Other planes, such as my Porterfield Collegiate, require the extra power of the 1200 mAh cells for their larger motors. But the Porterfield would fly with 800 mAh cells, and would probably get the same flight durations it's now getting, because it would weigh almost a pound less.

As a rule of thumb, I'd say use 800 mAh cells for 05 size motors and smaller. If your motor requires more than eight cells in the pack, use 1200 mAh sub-C cells. The larger motors are usually used in larger planes that can carry the extra weight of the sub-C cells and will benefit from the extra power. Planes with 05 and smaller motors will benefit from the reduced weight of the 800 mAh cells.

How Many Cells?

Motors are designed to require a certain voltage range. The number of windings of wire on the armature affects this. You will sometimes hear a motor referred to as "pattern wind" or "speed wind." This means that the armature is wound for special purposes, and you should stick with the battery pack and prop recommended by the manufacturer.

Most electric motors will handle voltages from 4.8V to 9.6V. Each cell can deliver 1.2 volts. This translates into packs containing four cells (4.8V), five cells (6.0V), six cells (7.2V), seven cells (8.4V), or eight cells (9.6V).

Four-cell packs are usually used for very small engines, such as 020 and 035 sizes. You'll sometimes find them in ready-to-fly airplanes like the small MRC Cessna. Since receivers require four-cell packs, it's possible to power both the receiver and motor from the same pack, saving considerable weight. But the motor has to be shut off before the pack is discharged far enough to affect control. The MRC Cessna does this with a very clever motor control circuit that senses the voltage of the pack. It gives you two to three minutes of engine run, then shuts the engine down with plenty of power left over for a long glide home.

Five-cell packs used to be common in some RC cars. They aren't used as much anymore, since the common motors used in cars (the Mabuchi RS-540) runs better on six or seven cells.

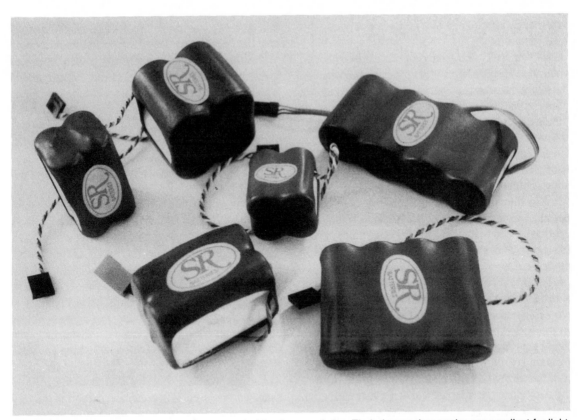

SR Batteries makes battery packs in every conceivable shape and size. Their tiny receiver packs are excellent for light-weight RC models. The larger packs are widely used to drive electric motor systems. SR packs are available wired with your choice of connector, or solder on your own. (Photo courtesy *Model Retailer* magazine)

Six-cell packs are available in several different configurations. Put together in two sticks of three cells each, they're used in many RC cars. Other cars use a "hump" pack, five cells side-by-side with a sixth resting on top, slightly to one side. These are inconvenient for airplane use, but some planes are big enough to take them. You can sometimes open the pack up and resolder the top cell in a more convenient position.

Seven-cell and eight-cell packs are almost always put together side-by-side. This makes it easy to slide them in and out of narrow fuselages. Sometimes you'll find the cells stacked together in a block, designed to fit a space in a sailplane fuselage.

Making Up Battery Packs

You will probably want to make up your own bat-

tery packs sooner or later, or at least modify a standard pack. There are a couple of things you'll have to keep in mind to do it properly. First of all, the connections between the cells have to be really good. If you use thin wire, or solder the connections poorly, instead of a connection you'll have a fuse waiting to heat up and blow. Meanwhile, it robs your pack of power by warming up. That heat comes from current that ought to be going to the motor.

I try to find cells that have tabs stop-welded onto the terminals. When I make up a pack of these, I tin the tabs on the sides that will make contact with each other, and solder them together over a wide part of their surface. If the straps barely touch each other, don't try to solder them together; use a wire jumper.

Because of the way the straps are placed, you will have to make up the pack by soldering the cells together in pairs. Then you connect the pairs with wire jumpers.

If your cells don't have tabs welded to them, you can solder directly to the terminals, but be careful! Keep in mind that heat is the greatest enemy of ni-cad batteries. If you lay the soldering iron on the cell for a long time, you'll start to boil the electrolyte inside the cell near the terminal. This will quickly cause the cell to vent and lose capacity. Make sure that the iron is in contact with the cell for as short a time as possible.

Tin the wire and the cell terminal before soldering. I've found a product that makes this process a lot faster and results in a much better solder joint. It's called Supersafe Solder Flux, and it's available at your dealer or from Ace RC. Supersafe is a greenish liquid that comes in a small plastic bottle. I dab a drop onto the wire and terminal with a short wooden stick. When you touch the iron and solder to the spot where the flux is, there's a hiss as the flux heats up, and the solder instantly spreads throughout the wire braid or over the surface the iron has warmed. Supersafe flux has made soldering a lot easier for me, and I use it everywhere for electrical soldering.

Once you have some solder stuck to the battery terminal and through the braid of the wire, it's very easy to make a good solder joint. Touch the wire to the terminal, and heat the wire with your iron until it melts the solder on the wire, then on the terminal. Remove the heat as soon as this happens. Keep the wire still until the solder sets. You might find a handling fixture very useful for this. You can make one of these by soldering an alligator clip to a piece of flexible solid wire and setting it in a heavy base. The clip holds the wire. I use a neat little fixture from Polk's Hobbies that has two alligator clips and a magnifying glass mounted on a heavy metal base. It cost only $5, and it's saved me a lot of effort. You can get Polk's products at your hobby shop, or order directly from their ads in the model magazines.

Once you have pairs of cells soldered up, lay them out in the configuration you want and secure them with one wrap of black electrical tape. I like this tape because it can be stretched tight and will hold the cells firmly. Then do the final soldering that makes the pairs into a pack. Finally, attach the power leads to the positive terminal of the cell at one end and the negative terminal of the cell at the other end. You should cut one lead long enough to go to the back of the pack, so both leads will come from one end of the pack and be of equal length. When the leads are connected, you can tape the long lead against the side or the top of the pack. Finally, put a layer of electrical tape over the terminals on each side of the pack. This is very important. If you don't insulate the terminals, you could get a direct short between several cells if the pack comes in contact with a metal surface.

A pack put together this way will be strong, but sometimes you'll need it to be stronger. I always encase homemade packs in heat-shrink tubing. You can buy lengths of heat-shrink tubing as wide as four inches. It shrinks quite a bit, so you can use a piece that's oversize. Cut it oversize so that the ends will cover the cells at either end. Slip it over the pack, and shrink it with a covering iron or heat gun. You can use a soldering iron or a match to shrink the tubing, but you will probably melt through it in a couple of places before you're through. You'll get much more even shrinking by using the wider surface of an iron.

Wire

The wire you use depends on the size of the cells in the pack and the amount of current you expect the pack to put out. Thin hookup wire is fine for receiver battery packs, but is a very poor idea for electric flight packs. The best wire you can use is silicone wire. Several companies sell this wire, including JoMar, Ace RC, and SR Batteries. It is very flexible, and will easily carry just about any current you'll encounter in electric power systems.

Silicone wire is a fairly loose braid of a lot of fine wire, so it's very important to use a wire stripper to get the insulation off the ends. If you cut too deeply, you'll be losing a lot of the current-carrying capacity of the wire. If you use a solder flux such as Supersafe, the solder will wick through the wire braid quickly and you won't have to apply as much heat.

Connectors

When the pack is wired, you want to choose the connector you'll require. I use three-pin Deans connectors for smaller packs. I wire them with the positive wire to pin #1 and the negative to pin #2, and leave pin #3 empty. This way if the plug gets inserted backwards (which isn't easy, but can be done), no connection will be made.

Astro Flight and Leisure Electronics, the two biggest suppliers of electric flight systems in the United States, use small Molex connectors. These are impossible to hook up backwards, and will carry all the amps you need.

When you begin to attach the connector, remember that you can short out the entire battery pack if the two bare ends of the power leads touch before you get them attached to the connector. Be extra careful as you trim these leads to length, strip them, and trim them. I usually strip and tin only one lead at a time, then attach it to the connector before even stripping the other lead. This minimizes the chances of shorting.

Larger connectors such as the Molex plugs will come with the metal contacts on a strip, separate from the plastic connector body. Even if these look like crimp connectors, you should always solder them in place. Once they're in the plastic plug body, it's very difficult to get them out again!

When you make up one of these connectors, first check the polarity of the wires and connectors you'll be using. Male and female connectors go in different plugs. It may seem obvious, but it's very important to work it out beforehand; correcting mistakes will *not* be easy! Tin the wire with liquid flux as described above. Bend the thin metal terminal lugs around the tinned wire to hold it in place, then apply a little heat from your soldering iron and the solder will flow into the connector. Now push them into the connector body until they click into place.

You should always use female connectors on battery packs. Many male connectors, especially the common Deans type, have exposed pins. If these touch something metal, such as the body of your car, they'll cause a direct short.

Sermos Connectors

A small company called Sermos RC has introduced a unique connector to the market. It's a heavy-duty industrial type, designed for tens of thousands of connect-disconnect cycles. It also has the unique feature that the individual poles of the connector can be configured any way you please: stacked vertically or horizontally. The two poles slide together with clips on the side of the pole body. So, if you want to be certain that you don't plug a pack in backwards, you can rotate one pole 90 degrees to key it to its connector.

These connectors are so sturdy and practical that I think they will become the standard for large battery packs. Right now, "standard" Molex-type connectors are the most common, since they are used on most RC car batteries. But the Sermos connectors are becoming popular among serious electric fliers. It won't be long before packs and motors are available with these connectors. Meanwhile, they are very easy to wire into your system yourself.

ENGINE SELECTION

If you're building a kit, I strongly advise sticking with the recommended power package. If you've got a standard airplane and are contemplating converting it to electric power, it isn't so simple. Weight is the important factor in determining your success.

Bob Boucher of Astro Flight has a simple rule of thumb: Weigh the empty airplane, then look for a power package that comes closest to that weight. You can go a little over, but not as much as, say, 10 percent of the total weight of the airplane and power system. This still gives you plenty of latitude.

Note that I'm talking about *complete* power packages here. It's important to consider the total weight, since the batteries are the heaviest part. It's also very important to be sure that the motor is designed for the battery pack you plan to use. Thanks to the popularity of RC cars, there is a large selection of motors available that are wound differently.

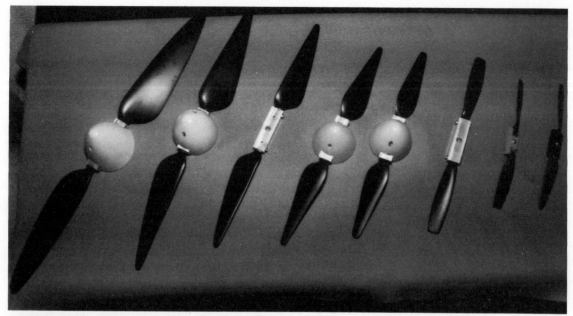

A complete line of folding props designed especially for electric flight is offered by Sonic-Tronics. The smaller ones are for direct drive, and the larger will work well for geared motor systems. Several include a custom-made spinner. (Photo by Holly English Payne)

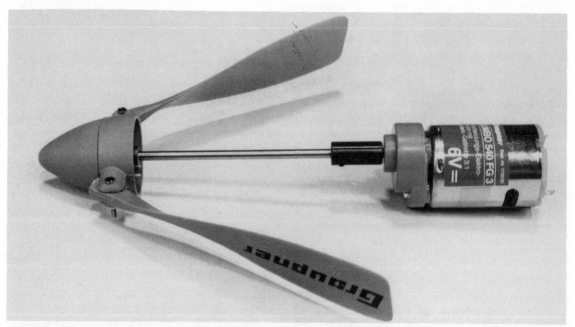

Graupner electric flight systems are imported by Hobby Lobby International. This one uses a prop shaft extension that allows you to put the motor closer to the plane's center of gravity, and have a long enough nose to use the folding prop. (Photo courtesy *Model Retailer* magazine)

This means that the amount of wire wound onto the motor armature varies with the intended application of the motor.

Any motor is a compromise. If it is wound to give maximum speed or torque, it will have relatively high power consumption and shorter battery life. If wound for the longest battery run, it won't deliver as much speed or power.

In everyday operation, this means that you should be aware of the battery pack your motor was designed to be used with. Don't take a motor out of an off-road racing buggy and expect to get the same performance as a motor wound specifically to turn a prop! It'll work, all right, and it's a good cheap way to get started. But the motors that are custom-wound for airplanes will work better.

PROP SELECTION

If you're using a gas engine, you can play with the size and pitch of the prop you use. Not so with electric power. There is usually a specific prop (or two at the most) that works well with one motor/battery/gear drive combination. You're safe sticking with the manufacturer's recommendations.

If you want to experiment, do it after the first few flights so you have a valid basis for comparison. Then go up or down an inch in pitch or diameter—one or the other, not both. Log your flight time and battery run time. Now charge your battery, slap on the recommended prop, and fly. Log this flight, made under the same conditions as the one with the experimental prop.

While you're experimenting, try different brands of the same size prop. Minor differences in pitch angle, blade width, and so on can make a difference in your flight performance.

People have used folding props for a long time to improve the airplane's glide. That prop sticking

Bill Winter checks the control linkages on his Heron before another flight. The Heron has a long prop shaft extension to allow the use of a folding prop. It climbs fast, and when the prop folds back, the glide is beautiful. (Photo by author)

motionless in the wind creates a lot of drag. Even worse is a windmilling prop. When a prop is being spun by the wind and not its motor, it's using up energy. It makes a very effective brake!

A prop with blades that fold backwards against the nose of the airplane doesn't cause these problems. Forward motion of the plane folds the blades back when the motor stops. Starting the motor again unfolds the blades, and centrifugal force keeps them extended.

The only caution to keep in mind when using a folding prop is to make sure the nose of the plane is long enough! I know it might sound silly, but I speak from experience. The first time I tried a folding prop it was on one of my old faithful electric jobs. The prop folded beautifully when I stopped the motor. When I started it up again, one prop blade chopped a neat slice through the leading edge of the wing.

Robbe makes a series of folding props designed for their geared motor systems, including the only three-bladed folder I've seen. I've had very good success with them. Windsor Propeller makes a folding prop in its Master Airscrew line that works very well on geared 05 size motors. Sonic Tronics is developing a whole line of folders—seven sizes ranging from 6-3 to 15-7. These props come with special hubs and spinners.

MOTOR CONTROL

You will almost certainly want to install some form of motor control in any electric plane you have. Even if the plane is a ready-to-fly job that comes without an on-off switch that's controllable from the ground, I strongly recommend installing one. One strong reason is that it gives you the ability to shut off the motor in the event of an "unplanned" landing. Stalling the prop against the ground or in high grass will pop the fuse quickly. If there's no fuse, it'll destroy the motor and battery pack before you can reach it to turn it off!

Another good reason for installing a motor switch is that you will get much better flights. If you can use the motor to take the plane up to altitude and then shut off the motor and glide, your battery

pack will not have to work while you're gliding. That's that much more flying time.

I've had good luck with a very simple on-off switch. I use a microswitch with a leaf-type lever on the contact, bought from Leisure Electronics. If you find a microswitch in a local electronics store, be sure you get one that is rated to be able to take at least 20 amps of current. I solder the switch into one lead from the motor, between the motor and the battery plug, so that the circuit is complete when the switch is depressed. Then I glue the switch to the side of a small servo at an angle that allows the servo arm to hit the switch at one end of its throw. The easiest way to do this is to turn on the radio system and set the servo at full throw, and hold the switch against it in the proper position. Then run a little Super Jet into the joint between the switch and the servo body. Move the servo arm to the other extreme, and reinforce the glue joint.

I prefer to use the throttle stick of a standard radio system for this on-off control. You could use a switched channel like the retract channel, but using the throttle is more natural and easier to remember.

There are several commercially available switches of this type. Some, like the Robbe and RAM units, mount a switch on a plastic piece that fits over the top of the servo. Astro Flight sells a unit that contains a relay and operates directly from the receiver, so no servo is needed.

SPEED CONTROLLERS

The ultimate in controlability for an electric plane is a proportional speed controller. These electronic devices allow you to "throttle" the electric motor with the throttle stick on your transmitter. If you're using a larger electric motor with a gear or belt drive system, you must have a speed controller. This is because abruptly switching on the motor can cause the gears to grind and the belt to slip!

Many speed controllers incorporate a relay at full throttle. This is a desirable feature because the circuitry of the speed controller absorbs some of the power going to the motor, even at full throttle. If the controller has a relay, it can use it to completely remove the controller from the circuit when you sig-

This electronic speed controller for electric models is made by JoMar. They make several models for different sizes of engines and battery packs. A speed controller allows you full proportional control rather than just engine on-off. (Photo courtesy *Model Aviation* magazine)

nal full throttle. This makes the power loss an absolute minimum, giving you more speed at full.

Some speed controllers allow you to set the point at which this relay kicks in. With a smaller plane, you could set this point at, say, two-thirds throttle. This will allow you to be certain that the motor is getting full power. A larger plane will require more precise adjustment of the motor speed, as you look for the right cruising speed. You will benefit by setting the relay trip point near the top of the throttle range. When I set up a plane like this, I set the relay trip point four clicks down from the top of the throttle stick travel.

I have had excellent results with speed controllers from JoMar Products. Several are available, depending on the size of the motor/battery combination you will be using. The newest JoMar units use circuitry that completely isolates the receiver connection from the drive circuitry. This means that interference generated by the motor can't travel back through the controller into the receiver. This

"optical coupling" is an excellent feature to look for when you select a speed controller.

Some speed controllers designed for RC cars will work very well in airplanes. Bear in mind, though, that they're likely to be heavier than units designed specifically for airplanes.

RUNNING THE RECEIVER
FROM THE DRIVE BATTERY

Many speed controllers have what is coming to be called a "battery eliminator circuit." This is a circuit that reduces the voltage of the drive battery pack to something that the receiver can run on. You'll see this feature quite a bit in speed controllers designed for cars.

It's an excellent idea, but it can bite you, too. When the drive battery gets run down, the voltage drops. The receiver will lose the voltage that it needs very quickly. This isn't as important to cars, which won't do any damage if control is lost from

Woody Blanchard holds his scratchbuilt Liberator bomber, powered by electric motors. Multiple electric motors are easy to synchronize—just run them all from the same battery pack! (Photo by author)

a flat battery; after all, they'll just stop. But if your plane loses its receiver, you have troubles. Shutting off the motor will often let the battery pack "rebound" up to a voltage high enough to power the receiver, but what if you need a touch of power to land on the field?

The answer is to carry a very small receiver battery. During normal flying, there's plenty of power available to the receiver and the small battery never has to put out any power. When the drive pack goes flat, you have enough power from the small battery to get you back on the ground.

A battery pack as small as 100 mAh will do the job nicely. In my Leisure Electronics Senior Playboy, I carry a 50 mAh battery pack made by SR Batteries. This pack weighs almost nothing, around half an ounce. I can fly the Playboy all day and not need to recharge it. The Airtronics speed controller I installed in the Playboy was an ounce heavier than another unit I could have used, but I'm saving at least five ounces by using the tiny SR receiver pack instead of a standard 500 mAh pack.

SWITCHES

You will want to install a switch between the bat-

tery pack and motor. Be aware that not all switches are suitable for use in electric power systems.

Some motors we use can draw more than 30 amps. That's a lot more current than many small switches are designed to take. Even if the switch can handle the power, it might be on the ragged edge of getting too hot. A hot switch is soaking up power that ought to be going to your motor. My practice is never to use a switch that wasn't sold specifically for electric flight use.

Switches get vibrated a lot, and they get dirt and grit inside them. They wear out over time. You might not notice it right away, but if your favorite electric job isn't getting the flights it got when it was young, suspect the switches. Try measuring the rpm with a tachometer. Then connect the battery pack directly to the motor without the switch in between. If you see a gain of 100 rpm or more, replace that switch!

ELECTRIC KITS

Let's take a close look at several of the kits on the market that are specifically designed for electric power. This is hardly a complete list; new kits are being added all the time. But by reviewing this representative sample, we'll be able to get a good idea of what kinds of kits are available and what features they have. It'll also give us a chance to discuss special features of airplanes that are designed for electric power.

Astro Flight Porterfield Collegiate. One of the first electric-powered airplanes I ever built was the Porterfield Collegiate from Astro Flight. Five years, two motors, and three different battery packs later, it's still one of my favorite planes.

The Porterfield is a big airplane, with a wingspan of around six feet. I like this, since fliers who are uninitiated to the joys of electric power tend to think that all electric planes have to be small. The motor is completely covered by a plastic cowl, so the Porterfield looks like any other plane unless you're looking right in one of the holes in the front of the cowl. If there are people at the flying field who haven't seen the Porterfield before, I'll sometimes carry it out to the end of the runway and point it into the wind, then walk back to the pilot line. Someone always asks if I need help starting the engine.

The Porterfield is a close relative of the Piper Cub; it's frequently mistaken for one. It's a little slimmer in the fuselage than a Cub, and the rudder is a bit different. The prototype was usually painted red, with a white trim stripe straight down each side. It's a very simple color scheme to duplicate.

Since an electric airplane doesn't throw oil all over the place, you can cover it with tissue or light cloth and not worry about fuelproofing it. I covered the Porterfield with Super Coverite, which is lighter than the prepainted Permagloss Coverite. Super Coverite is a spun and woven fabric. It's the easiest covering material to apply that I've ever used. Since it's so light, seams caused by overlapping the covering almost disappear. Instead of having to stretch around a curve or a wingtip like plastic coverings, Super Coverite rearranges its weave to conform to the surface. To top it all off, it looks like the same cloth they used to cover the original Porterfield.

The kit comes with a plastic cowl that has to be painted. I found that a company called Fiberglass Master makes a cowl for the Astro Porterfield, so I ordered one. I like it better than the stock plastic cowl because it's more rigid and easier to work with. Instead of trying to find paint that matched the covering I used, I simply ironed the Super Coverite right onto the fiberglass cowl. Fiberglass Master makes cowls and wheel pants for hundreds of popular kits, and can do custom orders.

Construction of the Porterfield is like a very large Peanut Scale ship. You make up side frameworks over the plans and join them with crossmembers. It's easier than building a stick-and-tissue plane, though, because the sticks are ¼ inch square balsa. The firewall requires a little extra attention, depending on what engine you plan to mount. I started out with an Astro 15 with a belt drive, and installed the plastic Astro radial motor mount. If you used a cobalt 15 or a direct drive 40 motor, you'd have to move the motor mount up the firewall to make sure the motor shaft comes out the hole in the cowl.

I mounted the batteries in the Porterfield's nose, just behind the firewall. The Astro 15 calls for 12 cells, so I joined two six-cell packs of sub-C (1200 mAh) ni-cads and wired them into the system. Since the plane had turned out a bit tailheavy, I moved the batteries farther forward to bring the center of gravity forward. I hate to use nose weight; why give a piece of lead a free ride?

If you don't have a charger that can handle 12-cell packs, it's a simple matter to charge the 12-cell pack as if it was two six-cell packs. I soldered two extra connectors to the pack, effectively splitting it. By plugging an ordinary charger into each of these connectors, I can get a quick charge at the field. The only thing to be wary of in a setup like this is to avoid charging only half the pack by mistake. When you fly, the current flowing through the discharged pack will reverse-charge it, leaving you with a very unhappy battery. You might be able to save it by deep-discharging and cycling the pack several times, but it's better not to do it in the first place.

The only weak point I found in the Porterfield kit was the landing gear. These are preformed wire, and they work fine, but they have a tendency to spread in a hard landing. As you build, I recommend reinforcing the lower fuselage structure around the landing gear attachment points. This will allow you to bend the gear back to the proper angle without tearing them out of the inside of the fuselage.

The kit specifies Trexler air wheels. Trexler wheels are inflatable donuts on wooden hubs. They're easy to work with and very lightweight, but inflating them is a chore. You might prefer to substitute a very lightweight set of wheels such as the ones made by Dave Brown Products or Ace RC. If you want to go with the Trexler wheels but can't find them, SIG Manufacturing is a good source.

I originally flew the Porterfield with a three-position speed control. This was simply a DPDT switch with a resistor wired across the poles in such a way that the resistor was in the circuit when the switch was in the center position. A tiny hole drilled in the handle of the toggle switch allowed me to connect it to a servo with a thin wire pushrod. Since the servo overdrove the switch and stalled at either end, I rigged the wire to pass through the hole and project out the other side. Then I put two small wheel collars on either side of the switch, spaced so that they would push the switch the way I wanted it.

The three-position motor control was okay, but I found that I was using too big a resistor for low speed and the Porterfield wouldn't maintain altitude at that motor setting. I tinkered with soldering resistors of different values to the switch and finally found a good one. But by then I was getting more and more interested in proportional speed control.

I've had a JoMar electronic throttle in the Porterfield for the last two years of its life, and I'm very pleased. I can adjust the cruising speed of the plane very easily with the throttle stick. The newer JoMar units are optically coupled, which means that no current from the motor can get near the leads from the receiver and cause interference. With the speed controller giving me the ability to pick the proper cruising speed, I can get consistent eight minute flights out of the big Porterfield, or shoot six touch-and-goes and still have enough power left to climb to altitude and glide home.

Davey Systems Le Crate. Davey Systems is a company that made its reputation with sailplane kits. It was a natural for them to get interested in

electric power. They have several electric kits in their line, including the Caliph low-wing trainer, semi-scale models of the Curtiss Robin and Brown Miss Los Angeles, and the Le Crate.

Le Crate is one of my all-time favorite airplanes. It was designed by Bill Winter, a true old master if there ever was one. I've had the privilege of flying with Bill for a few years now, and he's forgotten more about airplane design than I'll ever know. Bill has written more books than he can remember, and has been an editor of model magazines since the days of *Flying Aces* in the late 1930s. Bill got excited about electrics a few years back. After modifying a few gas kits for electric power and experimenting with different combinations, Bill decided that he had to design something strictly for electric. The result was Le Crate, and it has been redesigned several times into one of the finest flying electric jobs you can find.

Le Crate uses three channels for control, with generous rudder and elevator area. The stabilizer has a lifting airfoil, which allows the plane to fly ''on the step;'' in other words, instead of pointing its nose at the sky in a power-wasting climb, it climbs happily at a very small angle of attack. Le Crate has a relatively simple airfoil, and is very uncritical in building, but it maintains the excellent gliding performance an electric plane needs to log flights of 15 minutes and more.

The Davey Systems Le Crate kit is excellent. The pans are well-drawn, and no special construction techniques are necessary. While this is not a beginner's kit, a mature first-timer should be able to handle it. It makes an ideal first electric plane for someone who is already flying gas jobs. Construction is standard, with the wings and fuselage built over the plans.

One very nice feature of the Davey Le Crate (and the other Davey electric kits) is the motor mount. Most other electric kits are designed for a specific motor, and only that one will fit, or you have to carve or form a wooden motor mount around the engine you plan to use. Davey kits have a motor mount that is made from two plywood plates. The plates have triangle strips running down the sides, giving them a shape that will fit over the cylindrical

One of John Worth's many experiments with electric power resulted in this Le Crate powered by twin Astro 035 motors. The engine mount allowed the engines to be angled differently. It flew, but not as well as with a single engine. (Photo by author)

motor. Long bolts extend upward from the bottom plate, which is glued into the nose of the plane. To install the motor, you put it on the lower plate, slip the upper plate on the four bolts, and use wing nuts to clamp the motor in place between the plates.

This motor mount allows you to use different sizes of motors in the Davey kits, with easy interchangeability. Gear drives are no problem; they simply stick out of the front of the mount a little farther. Cobalt motors, which have brush housings sticking out the back of the motor case, are simple to install in this mount. And in the event of a crash, the ply plates will be torn out of the nose structure. This can be easily repaired, and is a lot better than a bent motor shaft!

Le Crate has been tried with many different motors, geared and direct drive. My personal favorite is the Leisure Electronics 3:1 gear drive setup, with a seven-cell pack of 800 mAh cells, and an 11-7 prop. But I've flown Le Crate with everything from an Astro Cobalt 05 on direct drive to a motor and battery pack taken from an RC car.

I made one minor modification to the Le Crate. I installed a hatch in the bottom of the plane, so I can swap battery packs without taking the wing off. I always go electric flying with three battery packs, so I don't have to sit around waiting for a plane to charge.

Le Crate flies smoothly and easily, and will thermal like a small sailplane. An on-off control is essential to enjoy the plane properly. Gliding characteristics are so good that you shouldn't require a speed controller; you won't need power to "cruise." Just go up to altitude, shut down, and glide around for a while. The nose of the Le Crate isn't long enough for the long-bladed (12 to 13 inch) folding props I like to use. It's a good idea to have some sort of system to stop the prop from turning, so it won't slow the plane down in the glide. Many modern on-off controllers have a circuit that puts an electrical brake on the motor when it's switched off. If you are using a microswitch attached to a servo, you can extend a length of flexible pushrod from one side of the servo output arm. Set it up so that it comes out of the firewall and sticks out into the prop arc when the motor is shut off. You can set it up so that when you pull back your throttle control to half, the motor shuts off. Then, when you pull the throttle back all the way, the flexible pushrod sticks out into the prop arc and stops it. When you do this, you should let the prop slow down before sticking the prop stopper out into it.

Goldberg Electra. One of the most popular electric kits on the market is the Electra, made by Carl Goldberg Models. Goldberg has become justly famous for their series of trainer airplanes. The Eaglet and Eagle have trained a lot of people to fly. The Gentle Lady glider continues to be an extremely popular kit as well. It was only logical for the Goldberg designers to take the Gentle Lady and add electric power.

Because of Goldberg's orientation toward the beginner, the Electra has an outstanding set of instructions. Every step is illustrated by photos, and there's plenty of information for the first-time flier. In fact, the Electra is intended to catch the eye of modelers who have been running RC cars. You can use the same battery packs and chargers that you need for an electric RC car in the Electra. The Electra is such an easy flier that if you can drive an RC car you can fly it successfully. Many car racers have built the Electra and realized that this was what they were practicing for all the time!

The Electra is sold in two versions. The standard version includes almost all of the hardware necessary for the kit, but no motor. The deluxe kit includes an electric motor, propeller, switch harness, and spinner. This isn't a bad way to go, to keep things simple. Since the Electra is designed for standard-sized 05 electric motors, there are several motors available for it. You can get slightly better performance out of the Electra by buying the standard kit and installing a Leisure Electronics motor and battery pack or an Astro Flight 05 Cobalt motor. Both of these motor systems will require a seven-cell battery pack, which is a good idea anyway, even for the motor that comes with the Electra. I found that the best battery pack for this airplane is a seven-cell pack of 800 mAh cells.

The instructions show you how to install a third servo that lets you turn the motor on and off from the transmitter. To my mind, this isn't just a convenience; it's essential. You will increase your flight time tremendously by being able to turn the motor on and off. It's also a lot easier to land when you feel like it, rather than having to wait until the battery runs down. Finally, if the battery is flat but the plane's still flying, the prop can windmill. This will make the motor act as a generator and put a reverse charge in your battery pack! Install that on-

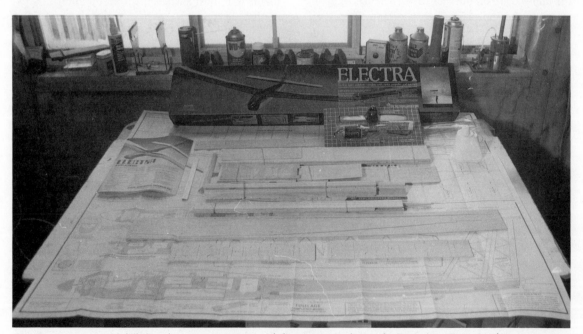

The Electra comes with full-size plans, and plenty of instructions to make it easy for beginners. This would be an excellent first airplane. It's available with or without a motor, prop, and spinner. (Photo by Jennifer Pratt)

An easy toss into the breeze and the Electra is airborne. If you install an on-off switch on the motor, you'll be able to get flights of 12 minutes and more. Fly up to a good altitude, shut off the motor, and when you get low, turn it on again. (Photo by author)

off servo and do it right from the start.

The Goldberg people very thoughtfully provide a switch harness with a fuse in it. Don't leave that fuse out when you rig your system. If the plane makes an "unplanned landing," the prop will be stopped against the ground. If the battery is still pouring power into the stalled motor, things can burn up very fast! The fuse protects the whole system.

When you fly your Electra, read the section of the instructions that describes the proper launching techniques. Launch the plane by pointing its nose straight out and level, not pointing up. When you take off you want speed. Remember, speed and altitude are interchangeable: Speed up, and you gain altitude. Let the plane build up speed, and you'll be able to trade it for altitude at any time.

The Electra is an absolute delight to fly. It has the best of the characteristics of the Gentle Lady. With the motor on, launch and cruise on up to altitude, then shut down the motor and glide around. You can turn very tightly if you add a little bit of up elevator in the turn; you'll soon get the technique down. Try different battery packs. I think you'll find,

as I did, that the Electra really prefers seven-cell packs and gives very satisfying flights with them.

Leisure Playboy. One of the first electric kits to hit the market in a big way was the Senior Playboy from Leisure Electronics. The original Playboy was produced by Cleveland Models, a company renowned for their airplane designs. The Playboy had a very high-lift wing and an airfoil-shaped tail. It was an ideal combination for electric power.

The Leisure Playboy kit itself is very good. It's not for beginners, because the Playboy design has some advanced features. The wing is undercambered, meaning that the underside is actually concave in shape rather than flat. This is great for lift, but is tricky to build and even worse to cover.

The Playboy kit plans are thoroughly detailed. They show an alternative cabin-style fuselage. I built the cabin version, since I liked the looks of it. As it turned out, it gave me a larger fuselage to experiment with different battery positions.

The Playboy's drive battery is located under the wing. A hatch is fitted to the bottom to allow you to get at the battery and radio gear. The engine is mounted to the ply firewall with bolts that go through the gearbox case. This is assuming that you use the Leisure gear drive unit, for which the plane is designed; you can use other units with very slight modifications. The nose itself is a balsa block that + hollowed out to clear the gear drive and glued to the firewall. It's easy to round it to shape with a sanding block.

You can build the Playboy wing in two different versions—dihedral and polyhedral. The dihedral version consists of two wing panels joined at an angle in the middle. The polyhedral wing has the two panels joined at a shallower angle, and smaller tip panels joined to them at about half their length out from the fuselage. I haven't noted any difference in flying characteristics between the two, and I found the dihedral wing easier to build and cover; there's less measuring to do. The wing ribs are all hand-shaped and sanded, a very nice touch. Follow the instructions closely when assembling it.

I tinkered with the battery position in the Playboy until I came up with an easy system for interchanging the packs on the flying field. I left the hatch

17

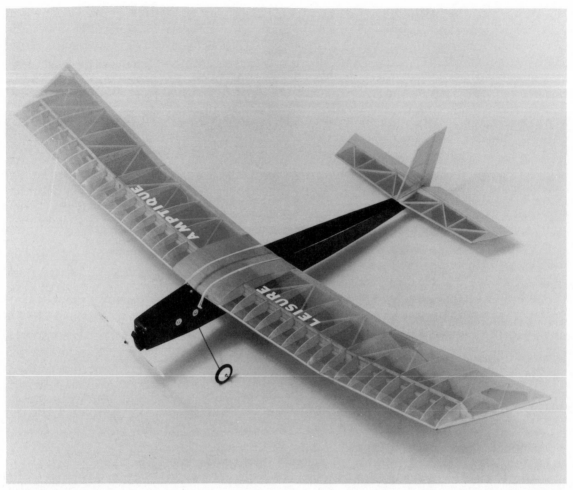

The Leisure Amptique isn't really an Old Timer, although it could be; the lines and construction are very similar to classic models like Leisure's famous Playboy. The Amptique is much easier for a beginner to build. The fuselage is made of die-cut sheets, and the engine mounts flat to the front of it. It flies beautifully. (Photo courtesy *Model Retailer* magazine)

off the bottom, so there's an open hole. I built a framework out of ¼ inch square balsa that fits a typical battery pack, and glued this into the fuselage. It's open on one end, and fits into the fuselage at an angle, so one end is up by the windshield and the open end is at the bottom, just barely sticking out of the hole in the fuselage. A rubber band is doubled over the bottom of the framework, so I can slip the battery pack in and out and slip the rubber band over it to hold the pack in place.

This setup allowed me to try different battery packs, and also to remove an old pack and insert a fresh one with ease. I found that I could get slightly

better flights out of a seven-cell pack of 800 mAh cells than I could with a six-cell pack of 1200 mAh cells. Even though the 800 mAh cells store considerably less power than the 1200 mAh cells, they weigh much less and so the plane is more efficient.

I started out with a simple on-off switch to control the Playboy's motor. After a few flights, I installed an electronic speed controller. The controller I used is an Airtronics unit intended for RC cars. It weighs an ounce and a half more than the servo and microswitch I was using, but it saves weight in another area. It has circuitry to supply power to the receiver from the main drive battery pack. This doesn't' mean that you can get along without a battery pack on your receiver, but it does allow you to use a very small receiver pack, since the receiver only draws power from it when the drive battery is flat. I put in a 100 mAh pack from Ace RC, and wound up saving ½ ounce of weight.

The speed controller has allowed me to make some very interesting flights with the Playboy. In calm air, I can throttle back and tool around at low altitudes. I can really stretch the battery run, getting up to 12 minutes of power thanks to the efficiency of the Airtronics controller. One of my favorite tricks is to see how slowly I can fly the Playboy. I gradually reduce the throttle while adding up elevator trim. When the Playboy's nose drops, I'm at the point of a stall and I add a couple of clicks of throttle. At this point the plane is perfectly controllable, and flying so slowly I can walk along next to

it and pluck it out of the air. You can see why I enjoy flying this plane so much!

RPM Snark. One of my favorite electric jobs is a ready-to-fly plane, the Snark 5T from RPM. It's sold widely in hobby shops, and is available mail-order from Hobby Shack. There are not many ready-to-fly electrics, and the others that I've seen are designed for the motor and battery they come with, leaving you no room to experiment. Not so the Snark. Its motor mount is a wooden tray; you hold the motor in place with rubber bands. You can strap in a wide variety of motors. Direct drive motors are the best to use for this plane, but you could easily fit a gear drive unit, especially one with a thrust line close to that of the motor, such as the unit sold by Davey Systems.

The Snark kit is a dream to put together. When you open the box, you find a completely built fuse-

The Snark 5T is almost-ready-to-fly. Mine took just over three hours to assemble. It's an excellent performer, capable of eight-minute flights. Engine and battery are not included. (Photo by Jennifer Pratt)

lage, two wing halves, and a rudder and elevator that are built and hinged to the fin and stabilizer. You join the wing halves with the included epoxy glue. Then you glue the tail surfaces on the plane and slip the control rods through the tubes that are installed in the fuselage. The wire landing gear are bent to shape, and you fit them into the wooden block on the bottom of the fuselage and hold them in place with screws. Rubber band your motor in place, glue together the two halves of the cowl, and mount it in place over the motor with small screws. Now install the radio. You're ready to go flying! It took me a total of three hours to have a plane that was ready to go to the field and enjoy.

The Snark has a wooden cavity on the underside of the fuselage for the drive battery. I cut a small hole in the front of this and stuck the plug from the motor switch through the hole. To install the drive pack, I connect it to the plug, push the connected plugs back through the hole, and fit the battery into the cavity. It fits tightly enough that you really don't need anything to hold it in. The kit includes a little plywood piece that is intended to hold the battery in; it screws into the front of the battery cavity, and swings out of the way when you want to change batteries. I found it completely unnecessary.

The Snark is a hot flier for an electric plane. It's fast and snappy, much closer to the performance of a small gas plane than the slow, stately Old-Timers or sailplanes that you usually see with electric motors. I tried different motors and batteries, and finally settled on a Mabuchi 550 motor turning a 9-6 Top Flite nylon prop. The Mabuchi 550 is similar to the motor sold with the Goldberg Electra, and is also found in some RC cars. Many hobby shops sell them as replacements for cars. I can get seven minutes on a six-cell pack of 1200 mAh cells, like a standard RC car pack, but I can add a minute to those flight times by using a seven-cell pack of 800 mAh cells. There's plenty of power to take off from smooth ground. Use the rudder to keep it straight, and it will fly off the ground with no up elevator necessary. This takes some power, so you will increase your flight time by a half a minute or so by hand-launching the Snark. It's easy to launch; I usually do it standing still.

This delightful plane currently lives in my office. I look at the weather at about 10 in the morning, and if it looks good, I start charging batteries. By the time lunch rolls around, I have three peak-charged drive packs, and I'm off to a nearby park for a pleasant hour of flying. That's another advantage of electric flight: convenience!

PREVENTING MOTOR INTERFERENCE

Electric motors cause radio interference. There's a lot of sparking going on between the

The MRC electric Cessna Skyhawk is an almost-ready-to-fly kit. Made from lightweight molded foam, it comes with the motor already mounted. The kit includes a battery pack and charger, and spare gears and prop. (Photo by author)

brushes and the spinning commutator. Fortunately, you can trap all that electrical junk before it gets near your receiver.

You should always have capacitors on the motor itself. Almost all motors come with these already in place. Take a look at them. There's a small capacitor soldered to each terminal. The other lead of each capacitor is soldered to the metal case of the motor. This effectively traps most of the sparks from the engine. No matter what sort of speed controller (if any) you use, you must have these capacitors in place. Some motors also come with a much larger capacitor soldered to both motor terminals; this is helpful but not essential.

Speed controllers can be a conduit for motor interference. After all, they are connecting the motor and battery pack directly to the receiver! Some sort of electronics to trap motor interference before it travels back through the controller to the receiver is necessary.

The earlier speed controllers often came with a large diode that was installed between the controller and the motor. This prevented current from traveling back to the controller from the motor. This was a good fix, but the new optically coupled speed controllers are much better yet. JoMar has gone to this kind of isolation, as have several other suppliers. Optical isolation uses a chip to keep the electrical system connected to the receiver completely separate from the circuitry connected to the motor. You might find that these "opto-isolated" or "optically coupled" controllers are more expensive than an old-style controller, but they're well worth it.

BREAKING IN ELECTRIC MOTORS

You might not expect it to be true, but electric motors require a break-in period just like internal combustion engines. This is not due to the bearings or the fit of the rotating armature to the magnets; they're built to very fine tolerances. Breaking in an electric motor is entirely a matter of getting a good fit between the brushes and the commutator.

The commutator is round—obvious, right? Well, the brushes that touch the commutator are usually flat. They really need to have a concave surface, so that more of the surface area of the brush touches

the commutator surface. You can buy engines with the brushes shaped like this; that's why those engines cost a lot more. But most of the engines you buy will have flat brushes.

The brushes are held against the commutator by springs. As the motor armature spins, the brushes wear to the same shape as the comm. The closer they get to the same shape, the more power they can transfer. So the obvious thing to do is to run the motor until the brushes wear to fit the commutator.

I like to do this by using a charger to supply power to the engine. You have to use a constant current charger, with adjustable current output. I connect the charger to the motor leads. The motor can be in the model, or secured in a vise. I fit a cut-down plastic prop to the motor, just to move a little air through the motor and keep it from getting warm; it's not necessary to put any load on the motor.

Once I have everything connected, I turn on the charger. I use a small block of balsa to hold the timer switch open; you want it to stay where it is, rather than click to trickle charge. My balsa block is sized to fit between the charger knob and the edge of the charge meter; twisting the knob slightly lets me wedge it in place. Now, with the charger stuck in the fast charge mode, I can use the current adjust knob to vary the speed of the engine. I don't worry about how fast the motor is running, as long as it's turning up to near the speed at which it'll run with the flying prop on it. Once the motor is whining away, I leave the whole setup on for a couple of hours. This is enough to wear the brushes down until they fit the commutator nicely.

Of course, what you're doing is wearing parts of the motor, which does shorten its lifespan. Make sure that your motor doesn't come with the brushes already broken in. If it does, this exercise will simply shorten the life of the motor slightly. Many modern engines come with removable brushes; you can always take them out and see for yourself whether or not they need breaking in.

BATTERY CARE AND FEEDING

Ni-cad batteries are remarkable little jewels. They put up with a lot of abuse and continue to work

Joe Utasi proudly shows off his Astro Cobalt 40-powered OMAC. Joe owns JoMar Products, which makes electronic speed controllers that allow you to "throttle" your electric motor. (Photo by author)

fine. Unlike lead-acid batteries, which will degrade chemically if they're left at a state of partial charge, ni-cads aren't bothered by long periods of storage with little or no charge in them.

There are two enemies from which you should defend your ni-cad packs. The big killer is heat. If a ni-cad cell gets too hot, it loses some of its efficiency. If it gets really hot, a little vent will open up and release some of the electrolyte from inside the cell. This can ruin the cell in short order, but it's a lot better than having the cell burst open!

Several things can cause a ni-cad pack to overheat. Ni-cads warm up in the process of fast discharging. Unless they're shorted out, this won't get them hot enough to do any damage. The biggest overheating problems come during charging, especially when you try to fast charge a pack that hasn't had the chance to cool down after it's been discharged.

The answer? Let a pack cool down after use. It should be just barely warm to the touch before you hook it up to the fast charger. Follow this rule and you won't have heat-related problems with your ni-cad packs. As I've mentioned before, I generally go to the field with three battery packs: one to fly, one to charge, and one to cool down.

The other enemy of ni-cad packs is called memory. This is a peculiarity of ni-cads that can shorten their life. When you continually discharge a fully charged ni-cad cell to a partially charged state and then charge it back up to full again, it will sometimes decide that that's all the power you expect from it and refuse to deliver charge past that point. This is caused by internal chemical shorts between the layers of metal inside the cell. Memory never happens if you discharge the battery packs all the way down to 1.0 volts per cell, then charge them all the way up again. This is just what we do in electric

The Lanzo Bomber is a classic free flight design from the late 1930s. Leisure Electronics has turned it into an electric-powered RC plane, for three channels: rudder, elevator, and motor on-off. It flies beautifully. (Photo courtesy *Model Retailer* magazine)

The Astro Viking is a classic Old Timer kit from Astro Flight, updated to take three channels of radio control and an electric motor system. Planes like this fly best with a geared motor system swinging a large (11- or 12-inch) prop. (Photo courtesy Astro Flight)

flight. So you should seldom encounter memory in your ni-cad drive packs; it shows up more often in transmitter and receiver batteries, which aren't run all the way down every time they're used.

CONVERTING GAS PLANE KITS TO ELECTRIC POWER

There are plenty of electric airplane kits on the market. But if none of them appeals to you, or you see a different kind of kit that you think would make a good electric model, it isn't difficult to work a conversion.

There are several things to bear in mind when considering a particular plane for electric power. Electric power systems have a lower power-to-weight ratio than gas engines. This means that given two systems that produce the same amount of power, an electric motor and batteries will weigh considerably more than an engine and full tank of fuel. This means that the plane you pick to electrify should be capable of performing the way you want it with this extra weight on board. You can buy an electric motor and battery pack that is as powerful as a typical model engine, but it will weigh much more, so you have to plan for this tradeoff.

Noted Electric expert Bob Kopski drags his Astro 40-powered Piper Cub in for a low pass over the field. Bob writes the Electric Power column for *Model Aviation* magazine. (Photo by author)

Wing area is a crucial consideration. The bigger the wing, the better. For example, I know of several people who have installed electric power systems in the Goldberg Piper Cub kit, with almost no modification, and gotten very good flying airplanes. Dave Peltz, the AMA District Vice President from California and a very experienced flier, installed an Astro Cobalt 40 with a gear drive in a Goldberg Cub. He made no attempt to reduce the weight of the airplane. Dave's Cub can make very snappy flights of eight minutes and more in length; the Cub does touch-and-goes, loops from level flight, and lovely axial rolls.

A plane like a Cub, a high-wing cabin job with lots of wing area, is an ideal prospect for electrification. High-wing trainer planes, such as the PT series from Great Planes, would also be excellent prospects.

If the plane you have in mind is a suitable type, there are things you can do to improve the performance. Keep in mind the rule that your plane should weigh no more than the weight of the motor and battery pack. This is often an impossible goal, but trying for it will improve your performance.

You can lighten a fuselage by cutting holes in the sheet sides, especially toward the tail. You can often replace plywood firewalls and fuselage doublers with balsa pieces. If you are building a kit with a ply firewall (which most of them have), you can use the firewall as a pattern to cut two pieces of 1/16 balsa wood to the same size and shape. Cut them so that one piece of balsa has the grain running in the opposite direction to the other. When you glue these two pieces together oriented cross-grain, you will have a very rigid, strong piece that is lighter than the plywood. Since you aren't going to install an oily, vibration-producing model engine on the firewall, you don't need the plywood.

There are several places where you shouldn't lighten the structure. Leave things as they are in the landing gear area of the fuselage. This is where you're going to put the battery pack, and you don't want this heavy pack going through the floor in a hard landing! I seldom change the wing structure, either. You can save some weight by substituting hard balsa for spruce spars, but your wing will be

Yes, it really is electric-powered! Keith Shaw's fabulous Gee Bee Racer is a remarkably good flier. In Keith's capable hands it flies inverted and knife-edge, and does other aerobatics. (Photo by author)

less rigid. Better to accept the weight of the wing along with the structural strength that the manufacturer designed into it.

One good place to save weight is the wheels. You can save several ounces on a model the size of the Cub by checking the weight of the wheels you plan to use. Dave Brown Products has an excellent line of lightweight wheels in a wide range of sizes.

Finally, I'd like to point out that your own experience will be your best guide in modifying stock kits for electric power. Build one or two of the electric kits that are available, and get a solid grip on

Bill Winter's Heron in flight. The Heron was published in *Model Aviation* magazine, and full-size plan sets are available. This is the best-performing electric the author has ever flow. (Photo by author)

battery charging techniques. You'll make much better decisions in the process of redesigning a gas kit for electric. When you feel you're ready, have at it!

CHARGING SYSTEMS

There have been *tons* of chargers sold over the past few years. Most of them have been sold through hobby shops, to people who have used them for charging RC car packs. Today there's a bewildering array of products available. How can you tell what's best for you?

Well, it depends on what you're going to use it for. One of the under-$50 units will be fine for some youngster starting out with his first RC car. But when you own more than two or three battery packs, you're going to need something that can operate all day. When you fly electrics, you want to get the absolute maximum charge you can into each pack.

Let's look at the most popular chargers that you'll find in your hobby shop.

While some chargers come with the ability to use house current for input power, most are intended for use with an auto battery supplying 12 volts and at least 5 amps. All the chargers available for car use require this input voltage and current as a minimum. Some chargers are more sensitive to the input voltage than others, but most can take 14 volts input. Manufacturers design their chargers to handle the overvoltage because people sometimes start their cars with the chargers still hooked up. With the engine running, the car's alternator can supply 14 volts. So this kind of abuse usually won't blow the charger; in fact, some chargers will operate happily with the overvoltage, and will put a faster charge into seven- and eight-cell battery packs with the car engine running.

So suppose you don't want to take the charger out to the garage to charge your batteries? You can get a 12-volt power supply from Leisure Electronics or Astro Flight. The Leisure unit is the one I prefer, because you can adjust the output voltage from about 9 volts to over 13. But neither charger will put out the amps needed for one of the chargers designed to charge more than eight cells, such as the Robbe Automax 21 or Astro Super Charger. One

of these chargers will just have to use a car battery, until someone comes out with a power supply that will put out more than 6 amps when the charger needs it.

Astro Flight. The company that originated electric flight offers a wide range of chargers. They're made in the U.S., and my experience shows that the quality is excellent. When I ran my temperature tests the Astro chargers had the hottest faceplates, but the transformers inside ran coolest of any I tested. The reason is obvious: The metal faceplate is used to dissipate the transformer's heat.

Three of Astro's five chargers are aimed at the car market. They are intended to charge six or seven 1200 mAh sub-C cells. Let's look at these first.

Thermal Cutoff Chargers. Astro Flight chargers model 101 and 102 are designed to charge six-cell sub-C battery packs only. Since this is the most common size found in RC cars, and these units are very competitively priced, they've been well accepted.

Before you ask, yes, any of these chargers will charge a seven-cell pack too. It will take longer—30 minutes or more—but it will be a full charge.

Instead of using a timer to prevent overcharging the packs, a heat sensor is rubber-banded to the pack before the battery is connected. The charger puts in fast charge current that varies with the internal resistance of the cells. It generally starts out around 4 amps, and will be less than an amp at the end of the charge cycle. The charger continues to deliver current until the heat detector senses a rise in cell temperature. When this happens, the charger switches to trickle charge. No controls or switches are necessary: All you need is a meter to tell you what current is going in, and a light to indicate trickle charge.

The meter will give you an idea of how the charge is progressing. If the charge current is above 3 amps, you're still in the first two or three minutes of charge. If the current is one amp or less, you're getting near the end of the cycle. In my tests, flat battery packs ran through complete charge cycles in 25 to 30 minutes. That's longer than a timed charge, but the charge is a certain 100 percent. In fact, it's an overcharge, but the thermal sensor prevents the overcharge from running away and damaging the pack.

One disadvantage of this type of charging is the fact that it really exercises the packs by consistently driving them into overcharge. Ideally, I think you should also have a charger that's capable of delivering a slow equalizing charge. Balance your packs with an overnight charge, and they'll be in better shape to handle the full charge these thermal cutoff chargers will give them.

Since these units depend on temperature, packs must be cooled to near room temperature before being connected, or they won't receive a full charge. This should be standard procedure anyway, since packs still warm from being discharged are physically incapable of accepting a full charge until they've cooled.

Astro ac/dc Charger. The Astro Flight ac/dc Charger has been the standard unit for both cars and airplanes for many years. There are good reasons for this. It's a simple, versatile, and durable unit that does anything that people need within the limitations of a simple timed charge cycle. It'll charge packs containing four through eight cells, of capacities from 100 to 4000 mAh.

The ac/dc charger is operable from either house

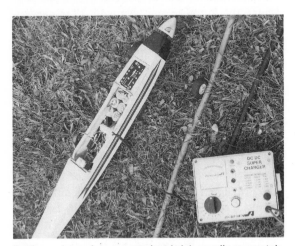

Putting a charge into a sport electric job usually means taking the wing off and plugging directly into the battery pack. The Astro dc/dc Charger will charge up to 20 cells from a 12-volt battery. Note that this plane has the Robbe speed controller mounted on top for better cooling and easy adjustment. (Photo by author)

current or a 12-volt source. It can easily handle the overvoltage from being connected to a car battery while the motor is running. In fact, to put a fast charge into an eight-cell pack, that overvoltage is recommended. When using house current, there's enough voltage to handle the eight-cell packs without doing anything special.

Both fast and trickle charge current is controlled with a knob on the face of the charger. For seven- and eight-cell packs, you bypass this control by turning the knob all the way to the right until it clicks. With the knob in this position, charge current is controlled by the amps provided by your input source and the internal resistance of the battery being charged.

The charger has jacks on the face to allow the easy connection of probes from a voltmeter. With a digital voltmeter hooked in, it's easy to get a peak charge by fast-charging until you see the pack voltage drop.

Astro dc/dc Super Charger. This newest charger from Astro is one of the most versatile units available. It will charge packs containing as many as 28 cells from a single 12-volt power supply. Or, it will safely fast-charge a single cell.

There's a switch on the face of the Super Charger that allows you to set two overlapping charge ranges: one to 14 cells, or 10 to 28 cells. Other than this, the Super Charger operates in an almost identical manner to the ac/dc charger described above.

When I tested it, I found that it lives up to all that's claimed for it. I had to scrape together every cell I had to make up a couple of 28-cell packs, but it really does charge 'em . . . in 15 minutes. And it'll charge 'em as fast as you can run 'em back down again.

When using the Super Charger with larger packs (over seven cells), I found that it's important to be aware of the current that you are supplying to the charger. A 12-volt power supply will run the Super Charger adequately for charging packs up to seven cells. A car battery is the best source for up to 16 cells; above that, I found it was easier to start my car and let the alternator pump more current into the charger.

If it could be operated from house current as well as dc power, the Super Charger would be perfect. That's possible, but it would price the unit out of sight. As it is, the Super Charger is the most all-around versatile unit I tested.

Leisure Electronics. Leisure was one of the first companies to introduce advanced chargers designed for the RC car trade. When they went into the aircraft business, they came out with one of the most versatile charging systems I've ever used: the Digital Charger and the 12-volt adjustable power supply.

The Leisure Digital Charger is a constant current charger with the charge current adjustable precisely, to the milliamp. The digital readout can be switched to display either the pack voltage or the charge current. When no battery pack is connected to the output, the voltage display shows the input voltage being supplied, so no meter is required on the power supply.

By setting the power supply to produce 14 volts, you can put a fast charge into an eight-cell pack. Set the power supply down to about 9 volts, and you can charge a single cell. By precisely adjusting the charge current, you can charge packs containing any common cells, from 100 mAh or less to 1200 mAh and above. You can also charge 4000 mAh cells, but it will take longer—probably about 45 minutes.

Leisure Car Chargers. Leisure makes a series of chargers that are primarily designed for cars but are useful for common electric flight packs. Leisure's #104 charger is simple and very inexpensive. It's designed to charge six-cell packs in 15 minutes, and has a 12-volt input only. The #105 will charge either six- or seven-cell packs; a switch selects the proper output voltage. It accepts only 12-volt input. The new #106 charger will charge six-cell packs in 15 minutes, or seven-cell packs in 20 minutes. It has the extra voltage because it uses house current for input. It's the only ac charger I've seen that can't also be run on 12 volts; this makes it simpler and cheaper. Finally, the #107 is the same as the #106, but can accept either house current or 12-volt input.

All four of these Leisure chargers have circuitry to discharge a battery pack and display the state of

discharge on the meter. The most common use for this feature is to flatten a partially charged pack so it will accept a full 15-minute charge. You can also use the Leisure chargers to balance a pack, since they all provide trickle charge current when the timer isn't operating.

Kyosho. Since Kyosho products have been available through Great Planes Distributing, they've appeared on lots of dealers' shelves and been very well received. Their most popular charger has been the #1848 Auto Charger.

The #1848 Auto Charger is a delta-peak detecting fast charger designed for input voltage of 12 volts only. It's capable of fast charging packs of any common capacity, from 250 mAh to 1200 mAh. Packs with more capacity than 1200 mAh can be charged, but it will take about 30 minutes. The Auto Charger will handle packs of from four to seven cells. It will also charge eight-cell packs, but again, it will take longer; the Auto Charger shouldn't be fed more than 14 volts of input power, and it takes about that to fast-charge an eight-cell pack. But for putting a fast charge in a transmitter on the field, the Auto Charger will do just fine. I tried it out on my Ace Olympic V transmitter, since I was sure the Sanyo 500 mAh cells in it would handle a fast charge. At just over 1 amp, the Auto Charger charged it all the way up to 13.2 volts, and cut off. Very nice!

This charger has two analog meters on its face, one for volts and one for amps. The ammeter only serves one purpose, to show the charge current. The voltmeter will show the input voltage of the supply battery, which is very useful to see if you have enough input voltage to do a good job of charging. During charge, this meter will show a voltage slightly higher than the battery pack. The voltmeter can be safely ignored during charge, since the automatic cutoff circuitry is monitoring the voltage much more closely than the meter can display. In fact, this charger cut off more reliably than any of the other peak detector chargers that I tested; it would trip at a drop of .02 volt, while ignoring the occasional fluctuation that a charging battery displays.

I found that the ammeter in the unit I tested actually displayed a current about .2 amps more than is being supplied to the battery pack. If the meter is going to be inaccurate, this is the side to be on. Supplying less current to the battery is definitely safer than too much current! And since the charger cuts off automatically, this slightly lower current does no harm to the charge.

The Kyosho charger doesn't come with a connector for the battery pack being charged. Instead, there is a very nice terminal block on the back of the unit. You make up a cord by stripping the wires from an appropriate connector and clipping them to this terminal block. Tinning the bare wires with solder is helpful. Since many battery packs (notably the Tamiya packs) come with wired charge connectors, this doesn't present a problem. But you will need a connector before you can use the charger.

Using the charger is simple. Hook up the source battery and turn the current adjust to full. Press the button, and the voltmeter shows you the voltage of the source battery. It should be between 12 and 14 volts. Turn the current adjust to low and hook up the ni-cad pack. Hit the button again, and turn up the current adjust to the spot shown on the ammeter for the pack you're charging. That's it; the charger will shut off when the pack is peak-charged.

In my tests, I found the charger performs very reliably. It charged six car packs without getting noticeably warm on the outside, and without overheating its transformer. As mentioned above, it charges eight-cell transmitter (500 mAh) packs adequately. I tried it out on an eight-cell 800 mAh pack, and it did fine after I increased the input voltage to 14 volts (using the Leisure adjustable power supply). The eight-cell pack took about 45 minutes to bring to a full charge.

The Kyosho Auto Charger has recently been upgraded and modified. The new unit is called the Lambda Charger. It has all the good qualities of the old Auto Charger and is used in the same way.

MRC. The company that put RC cars on the map and still dominates the field, MRC, has also produced a line of chargers. Originally they carried Tamiya chargers, which were not very impressive next to the Astro Flight and Leisure units. Several years ago, MRC started producing a series of chargers under their own label. I've used several, and they are good units.

One of the finest chargers I've ever used is the MRC RB-450. I don't think it's still available—a shame, since it does things other chargers don't. I've heard rumors that a similar unit might be on the way. Meanwhile, if you find one in a hobby store, give it a good look.

The RB-450 has a digital readout that can display the pack voltage before and during charge or discharge, and the current being drawn by a motor. A line of green LEDs shows the charge current; the first LED serves as a pilot light to show that the 12-volt input is connected. It will even display the input voltage so you can tell if your 12-volt battery needs charging.

The RB-450 will charge packs with from four to eight cells, and any common current capacity. You simply dial in a charge current appropriate to the pack. Charging eight cells will take a while, since the most input voltage the charger will take is around 13 volts. There are two charge modes: manual, which will charge until you turn it off, and auto, which will detect peak and shut off automatically.

In my tests, the RB-450 will reliably detect a peak at a charge current of .5 amps. This means you can peak charge a receiver battery on the field. You can use the same unit to charge a seven-cell sub-C drive pack in 15 minutes at a charge current of 4 amps. That's what I like in a charger—versatility.

MRC RB-475. The latest charger to come from MRC is the RB-475. It's primarily a car charger, intended for six- and seven-cell packs. It's a very attractive unit, and very attractively priced, especially considering that it's an ac/dc charger; it can run from house current as well as 12 volts. This is a strong convenience feature that a lot of modelers want.

The RB-475 delivers a timed charge with a 15-minute charger. The user can prevent overcharging a pack by testing it with the RB-475's meter and discharge circuit. Hook up the battery, select discharge, and watch the meter until the battery is discharged to the right capacity, illustrated on the meter face. Then throw the switch to charge and start charging. When the timer clicks off, the RB-475 delivers trickle charge current to equalize the pack.

A switch on the back of the unit selects output voltage for six- or seven-cell packs. Eight-cell packs can be charged in the seven-cell position; they will charge faster when the RB-475 is using house current, since more voltage is available. There are also two banana jacks on the end of the charger. These jacks can be used to monitor pack voltage with a digital voltmeter, or you can connect a battery that doesn't have standard Tamiya connectors through these jacks.

The 12-volt input comes with two connectors: a set of battery clips, and a cigar lighter plug. Some people prefer the plug, since there's no chance of reversing polarity and popping the charger; others like the clips, so they don't have to leave charging batteries inside their car. Both connectors plug into the 12-volt input line, which is fused.

In my tests, this charger ran very cool. I used it to charge six packs in a row, on house current, and it barely felt warm to the touch. The transformer ran cool, although not as cool as the Astro chargers.

It certainly didn't get warm enough to be in any danger of failing.

RAM. RAM was the first company to introduce heat detection as a technique to terminate charge at peak. Their Fool Proof Charger is now available in three models: dc input only, ac/dc input, or just the heat detector circuit for you to plug in between a conventional charger and your battery pack.

In my tests, the RAM Fool Proof Chargers ran coolest of any of the units I had. They're packaged in aluminum cases with lots of ventilation, and they have big, heavy transformers. These bruisers will go for days and never give up.

The ac/dc unit has a package of resistors potted in silicone rubber hanging off the charge cords. Putting the resistors in this package is one of the reasons the unit runs so cool. The package gets hot, though, and care must be taken that it isn't resting

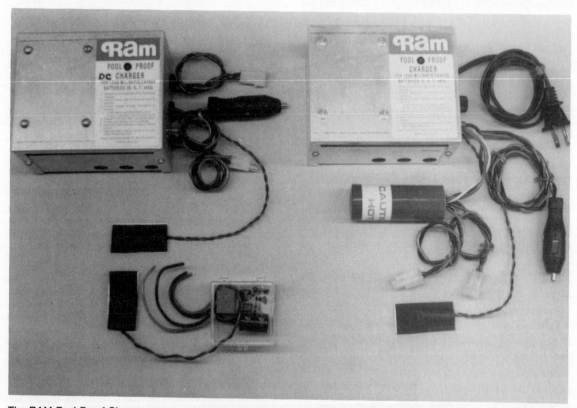

The RAM Fool Proof Charger uses a heat sensor to detect an overcharge. If the batteries warm up, the charger shuts off. At left is the 12-volt version of the Fool Proof charger; at right is the ac/dc version. In the foreground is the heat detector circuit, which is sold separately so you can use it with any charger. (Photo by Jennifer Pratt)

on something that can melt, such as vinyl dashboard trim.

The Fool Proof Chargers will charge five- or six-cell sub-C packs, or seven-cell 800 mil packs. The voltage of a seven-cell pack is just about the limit of its output, however, and it does it best when using ac house current. Of course, the heat sensing circuit could be put between any charger and any battery pack.

The problem I have with heat detection, as I've said before, is the difficulty of charging standard Tamiya packs with their thick plastic cases. By the time enough heat makes it through the case to trip the charger, the cells could be cooking off. I recommend using a shrink-wrapped battery pack with any heat detector charger, so the charger's sensor can rest right on the cells with only a thin layer of plastic between.

Robbe. There are two chargers in the Robbe line that are especially worthy of your attention. Robbe's chargers reflect the advanced German technology and European attitudes of the parent company in West Germany. They're very impressive.

Both of these Robbe chargers require a 12-volt power supply. They're designed to work with a freshly charged car battery. The Astro Flight and Leisure 12-volt power supplies will work as long as you aren't charging packs with more than six cells at fast rate, or seven cells at a lower rate.

Automax 8. The Robbe Automax 8 is the lower-priced of the two Robbe chargers I examined. It has an amp meter on the front with a wide scale and markings to show where common packs will read. Two slide switches allow you to select the amp-hour and voltage of the pack to be charged. The Automax 8 will charge packs of from four to eight cells, with cells of from 100 to 4000 mAh. The battery leads plug into two banana jacks on the front of the case. I like this setup, since it's very easy to make up sets of battery leads with the connectors your different packs use. The charger comes with a set of leads to the Tamiya-type Molex plug. Finally, there are two LED indicators on the face of the charger. The green one comes on to indicate a trickle charge, and flashes during the timer cycle. The red one lights to warn you that you don't have the switches set properly, or that something else isn't right.

The Automax 8 has a charge cycle that is unique in my experience. When you hook up a pack to be charged, it checks to make sure your switches are set properly and flashes the red Attention LED if it doesn't like the settings. The trickle charge comes on automatically at this point. When you push the Start/Stop button (it has to be held in for a few seconds), the Automax 8 feeds a fast charge current to the pack. It watches the voltage during this high-current phase of the charge. When the voltage gets up to a certain level (depending on the number of cells in the pack), the Automax 8 holds that voltage and lets the charge current taper off.

Since the pack has gotten a high-rate charge for the first phase, it's building up some internal resistance. So the charge current will decrease as the cell resistance rises and the voltage is held constant. When the current drops to half of the level it started at, phase three of the charging cycle begins as the Automax starts its internal timer.

The timer holds the charge current steady for 12 minutes. This is indicated by the flashing of the green Timer LED. When the time cycle is complete, the Automax 8 switches to trickle charge and the charge cycle is complete. Oh, I almost forgot: The Automax also senses ambient temperature and adjusts the charge current accordingly.

Now, that's different. Why go through all those gyrations just to charge a battery pack?

Well, I see this charger as a step above the timed fast charger, without the complications of a peak detection circuit. Peak detector chargers can overcharge and cook a pack, especially if the battery is warm to start with or it's a hot day. Plus, they're more expensive than the Automax 8. The Automax is a very good way to get a nearly 100 percent charge into a pack with absolutely no risk of burning up the pack; if it detects the high resistance of a too-hot pack, it won't allow higher than a trickle charge rate.

You don't often find a charger with the versatility of this unit: its ability to charge transmitters, receivers, cells as tiny as 100 mAh or as big as D cells. Add to this the unique charge cycle, and you have an excellent all-around charger for the serious car or airplane hobbyist. Electric fliers will especially like the Automax 8. Mine lived through several stress tests, including constant use during the '86 Keystone Electric Fly contest, and never did anything unexpected.

Automax 21. The Robbe Automax 21 is one of the most versatile chargers you can buy. Serious electric fliers have come to depend on the 21. I saw 15 of them at that 1986 Keystone Electric contest!

The Automax 21 has two features that have made it popular with electric fliers. First of all, it will charge a very wide variety of packs, from four cells to 21 cells and from 250 to 1200 mAh or larger. The charge current is fully adjustable. As with the Automax 8 described above, the battery connections plug into banana plugs in the face of the charger. You plug the positive lead into the common + jack. If you're charging from four to 10 cell packs, the − lead goes into the left jack; the right jack supports 11 through 21 cell packs. A meter shows the charge current in

amps, and a knob controls the amount of current delivered to the pack.

The other important feature of the Automax 21 is its peak detector circuitry. It is designed to monitor the pack voltage and stop the charge when it detects a drop, indicating the beginnings of overcharge. Peak detection is the preferred method of getting absolutely as much charge into a pack as it will accept.

The red LED indicator glows when the Automax 21 is connected to a 12-volt power source. When the battery to be charged is connected to the proper leads, you turn the current control to minimum setting and move the start/stop switch to Start. The Automax makes a peculiar whistling noise while it's charging, making it easy to tell when it has shut itself off. Now you dial in the amount of charge current you want. That's all there is to it; when the charger detects peak, it shuts off all current to the pack.

In my tests of the Automax 21, I've found its

At the Keystone Electric Fly, heavy duty batteries were on the field for people to hook their chargers to. Here you see several Robbe chargers, a RAM Fool Proof Charger, and a couple of homemade units. The hair driers are to blow air over the batteries to cool them. (Photo by author)

The Robbe Automax 21 is a very versatile charger, popular among electric fliers. It will charge packs of up to 21 cells from a 12-volt battery. The charger automatically detects peak charge and shuts itself off when the pack is fully charged. (Photo courtesy *Model Retailer* magazine)

detector to be the most sensitive of any I've tested. It will trip reliably before packs are overcharged enough to warm up noticeably, if the packs were cool to start with. The lack of a trickle charge circuit in the Automax 21 is a minus, but you can accomplish the same thing by setting a low charge current. The detector circuit works reliably at charge currents of ½ amp or over. So you can do a slow charge of, say, a 1200 mAh pack by feeding an amp of charge current into it and letting the Automax detect peak.

Hobby Lobby. Hobby Lobby imports the Graupner line of electric flight supplies from Germany. Most of these items are available to dealers, so look for them at your local hobby shop.

There are several chargers in the Hobby Lobby catalog. They're basic, useful units for car or electric flight use. I haven't had the chance to run any of them through my tests, but I have reports from two friends who use them and they're pleased with the performance and durability of the units.

One Hobby Lobby charger particularly caught my eye. This unit is an inexpensive, straightforward timed charger. Actually, it's two chargers in one: two timers, two meters, two outputs. When I go out flying electrics, I usually use two chargers since I have several battery packs. I can fly continuously if I can fly one pack, charge a second, and let a third cool down from use. But in order to use two chargers, I've had to carry a spare 12-volt gel cell to power one of them. This charger from Hobby

Lobby would save me that trouble, since its transformer is designed to keep two chargers going from one 12-volt input. The same thing will apply to car racers who have more than one battery pack—which is just about all of them.

Model Craft. Model Craft Manufacturing popped onto the RC car scene a year or so ago with a line of three "Pro-Tech" chargers at competitive prices. All three have some nice options and features. They include two 12-volt input cords. One is permanently fixed to the side of the case and has a cigar lighter plug; this is the one I prefer to use, since it's impossible to reverse the input voltage (which will quickly blow the charger). The other input cord has two medium-size alligator clips, and banana plugs that go to jacks on the face of the charger. The chargers also have banana jacks on the side, one to either side of the output cord, where you can connect a voltmeter to monitor pack voltage. Alternatively, you can use these jacks to attach a non-standard ni-cad pack to the charger. You can even use the supplied alligator clip cord for this. Of course, the charger comes with standard MRC/Tamiya battery connector.

All three Pro-Tech chargers have a discharge circuit and a meter on the faceplate. They all switch to trickle charge at the end of the timed fast charge cycle, indicated by a pilot light. You can get any of the chargers with either a brushed aluminum or black anodized faceplate.

This Twin Rapid Charger is sold by Hobby Lobby International. It will charge two separate battery packs of different sizes at different rates from a single 12-volt source—just the thing to keep you in the air when you have two or three battery packs! (Photo courtesy *Model Retailer* magazine)

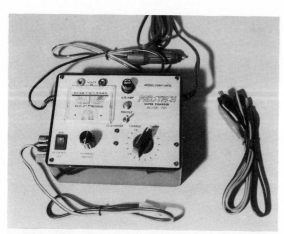

The Pro-Tech ac/dc charger operates from either a 12-volt battery or house current. Charge current is adjustable, and it will charge packs of up to eight cells. (Photo by Jennifer Pratt)

CHOOSING A CHARGER

When I evaluate a charger, I look for features that I need. Then I look for indications of the quality of the unit. The brand makes a difference; I've been using some brands for years and I know what to expect. I also measure how hot the thing gets after a couple of charges. If you don't hook it up to the source battery backwards, or short the output leads, you'll probably destroy a charger by letting it overheat. But a quality charger ought to be able to run for days under normal conditions without dying. If the instructions tell you to let the charger cool between charge cycles, that's a red flag; it shouldn't be necessary.

When I started testing, I put my temperature probe on the faceplate of each charger under test. The Astro Flight and Leisure chargers got the hottest; they would run up to 120 degrees and be there the next day after fast-charging all night. The RAM charger ran coolest. In between were the Robbe chargers and the Model Tech unit.

Then I opened the chargers up, and put my temperature probe on the transformer, which is the part most subject to heat destruction. Again, the Astro and Leisure units went up to 120 degrees and stayed there. So did almost all of the other units. The coolest running transformers are in the RAM and Robbe units, where there's plenty of ventilation. The surprise was the Model Tech units, where the transformers got above 150 degrees in a hurry.

The Astro and Leisure units use the metal faceplate of the charger to dissipate heat from the transformer. This can make you think that they're overheating, but it's very deceptive. I found that the Model Tech chargers, where the transformer sits in the plastic case by itself, feel cool on the outside but are getting really hot during use. You might consider drilling some vent holes in that plastic case to allow air to circulate through. In fact, this is a good idea with any charger that comes in a solid plastic case; one of the reasons the RAM charger ran so cool is that the sides of the aluminum chassis are open.

Chapter 2

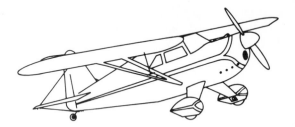

Advanced Radio Systems and Electronic Kits

RADIO SYSTEMS SEEM TO BE EITHER VERY SIMPLE and basic, or very complex. There's no middle ground. Once you've started out with a simple radio, you're likely to look at the bigger, more expensive systems as a logical next step. But do you *really* need all that stuff? Are these radios really any better than the simple, cheaper ones?

As usual, the answer depends on a number of factors. The complex radios are often specialized designs, intended mainly for aerobatics flying, scale models, or helicopters. If the models you want to fly fall into these categories, consider the fancy radios. If you're concerned about interference and want to put a radio in a valuable plane, you're going to have to pay for one of the more expensive systems. Let's take a look at some of the features you can get, so you can figure out which ones you want.

"BELLS AND WHISTLES"

Modern radio control systems are available with a dazzling array of functions and options. These are useful to the advanced modeler for specialized aircraft, but they can also come in very handy for sport fliers if you understand how they work.

Remember the second corollary to Murphy's Law: The more complicated something is, the easier it is to screw it up. Fiddling with those knobs and switches when you don't know what you're doing can crash airplanes. So can bumping them accidentally and failing to check that they're all where they belong. If you're using a tricked-out radio with controls all over the place, make it a habit to check the position of *each* switch before you start the engine. After takeoff, it's too late!

MULTIPLE FLIGHT PACKS

You probably started off with an inexpensive four-channel radio. Then you got another plane, and got another radio for it. Then the third plane came along . . . and so forth. You should consider buying new flight packs for your radio system, rather than a whole new radio.

A *flight pack* consists of a a receiver, a battery pack, and as many servos as the airplane needs. It's much cheaper than buying a whole new system, and it means you have fewer transmitters to lug to the field. It also allows you to pick the transmitter that feels best to you, and use it for more than one airplane.

On the negative side, it usually means that you are limited to whatever frequency the transmitter is tuned to. This can be annoying if you fly at a busy field, and there are lots of other people who use that particular frequency. One solution is to have a transmitter with a removable frequency module. You can buy a module on another frequency, and buy a flight pack with a receiver tuned to the second frequency. Changing planes is as simple as changing transmitter modules and frequency flags.

By now you should have a feel for what frequencies are always busy at your field. Many clubs log the frequencies that their members use, so they can advise you on relatively little-used frequencies if you're contemplating buying a new system or module.

Kraft Systems introduced a unique approach to the frequency problem a few years back: a synthesized radio system. Using a small screwdriver, you could adjust two controls on the transmitter and receiver to dial in any frequency you wanted. These units became quite popular, but have not been available since Kraft closed up some time ago. However, there is talk of other manufacturers introducing synthesized systems, and it may well happen soon. When they do appear, they will be compatible with the narrow band spacing that will be in place after 1991.

Personally, I prefer to use a modular radio design. I've finally settled on one transmitter that does everything I want it to, and I've customized it to my needs. Most of the airplanes I currently fly have flight packs tuned to this transmitter. It makes life a lot easier: one set of transmitter batteries to charge, one frequency to wait for, and one set of switches to look at! I'll go into more detail on this particular system later in the chapter; there are several others like it on the market, so you'll certainly be able to find one that fits your flying style.

The Module radios from Airtronics are loaded with advanced features. Mixing functions and switches are under the clear faceplate on the transmitter. The transmitter incorporates a timer and alarm. A special transmitter (right) is available with helicopter functions. (Photo courtesy Airtronics)

PREFLIGHT CHECK

Preflight checks are doubly important when you're using an advanced radio system. If you're using one transmitter for several airplanes, you will often change the controls—especially the servo reversing switches—for each plane. If you fail to check each time you fly, you can crash yourself quickly! I've made this such a strong habit that I do it every time I prepare for takeoff, even if I'm flying the same plane I landed a few minutes ago. It's a good habit to get into; I've occasionally spotted a developing problem that way.

The first thing to do, of course, is to get your frequency pin. Shooting someone else down by firing up a transmitter on their frequency while they're in the air can lead to terminal embarrassment!

The next step is to glance at all external switches and controls. You're thinking about the plane you're about to fly, so you know if it requires low rate, rudder and aileron mixing, or whatever. Check all switches, even the ones that don't do anything on that particular plane, and make sure they're where they should be.

Next, wiggle all the controls. Make sure they all move in the proper directions. I'm not suggesting that someone might have *deliberately* moved your servo reversing switches, but stranger things have happened. I once took off with the aileron servo reversed. Never again! So I stand behind the plane, where the sticks move in the same direction as the control surfaces, and check to make certain that the ailerons, rudder, and elevator all move the way they should. In fact, I sometimes throw in a little body English, swiveling my hips the way the plane will bank as I move the ailerons.

Then I go around to the front of the plane and check the throttle. Starting an engine that's at full throttle when you're expecting it to be at idle can be very dangerous.

With everything thoroughly checked out, I start the engine and taxi out. Once I'm sitting in takeoff position, I wiggle the air surfaces one final time. Now I'm ready to enjoy myself.

SUPER RADIOS

There are a number of radio systems that can best be described as "super radios." They typically offer you up to eight channels, and a host of other functions as well. You'll recognize some of them from lower-priced systems: servo reversing and dual rates, for example. But super radios go considerably beyond that.

The newest super radios incorporate microcomputer circuitry. They do this to offer more versatility in the way they're used, but it has an additional benefit. The components used in the rest of the radio have to be better in order to work with the microcomputer. So one of these computerized systems will have parts that are made to closer tolerances, and will perform better than standard systems. The tight tolerance is a large part of what you're paying for!

Let's take a look at some of the features that you can buy in a super radio, then we'll go in depth into one of the most popular systems. Like our reports on various kits in this book, looking at this system will help give you an understanding of all of them. The similarities are strong.

Simprop. The Simprop radio from Germany is being imported into the U.S. by Altech Marketing and sold through hobby shops. This is a thoroughly modern system with the latest microcomputer technology. It's a PCM system, so the receiver incorporates a computer that listens for the coded signal from its transmitter. A fail-safe feature is designed in. This means that if the receiver loses the signal from the transmitter, it holds the controls at the position commanded by the last clear signal. If more time goes by without a good signal, the receiver moves the controls to a preset position and reduces the throttle.

The Simprop transmitter is completely modular. Switches on the top can be positioned in several different holes, wherever you find them easiest to use. There's a 1200 mAh battery in the transmitter, more than enough for a long day's use. The frequency module is easily changeable on the field.

Four specialized modules are available for the transmitter. All provide servo reversing on seven of the 10 channels. The All Around Module gives you dual rate on the control surfaces, differential aileron control, programmable mixing of aileron and rud-

The Simprop PCM 20 is an advanced RC system that features interchangeable modules to change the functions. The modules snap into the lower faceplate of the transmitter. A complete line of accessories is available. (Photo courtesy Altech Marketing)

der, mixing of flaps and elevator, and complete options for flying V-tailed airplanes and planes with elevons. The Pattern Module provides all of these features plus adjustable retract throw, programmable snap flaps, and throttle trim disengage. The Glider Module has the same features as the All Around Module, plus a mixer for airbrakes and elevator, a switched function to configure flaps and ailerons for launching, a "speed switch" that moves the flaps to a preset maximum speed position, and a function that mixes flaps, aileron, and elevator all together.

Several unique accessories are sold for the Simprop system. One is a Frequency Monitoring Unit that lets you listen for possible interference sources.

Another is a quick charger for the transmitter and receiver batteries. Four different servos are available.

Futaba PCM Systems. Futaba was the first company to bring PCM transmission to the American market in a big way. Their line now includes several PCM systems, from the inexpensive Conquest to the top-of-the-line 8SGA.

The fancier Futaba systems allow you a great deal of versatility in options and functions. You can mix any channel with any other channel, select dual or exponential rates, and program different control settings for pushbutton maneuvers. You can mix flaps and spoilers, and tie them both to the throttle position. Unlike the other systems we've looked at, to program the Futaba super radios you remove the cover on the lower back of the transmitter. A small screwdriver is provided to help with the adjustment pots and switches.

Several Futaba super radios come with a very interesting accessory: the Tachotimer. This is a display built into the bottom front of the transmitter case. It shows the amount of time the transmitter has been turned on, and has several alarm and stopwatch functions. Plug in an optical sensor on a three-foot cable, and this display becomes a digital tachometer.

These systems have proven to be very popular. The fancy features can be turned off until you're

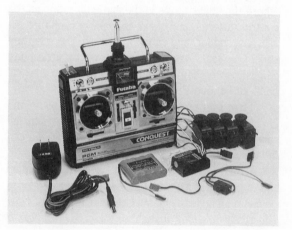

The new Futaba Conquest PCM radio system brings PCM transmission down to a sport radio price. It has all the basic functions: servo reversing, dual rate, and a retract channel. (Photo courtesy Futaba)

ready to use them, so you can get used to the system and work gradually into the high-level stuff.

JR Galaxy Computer 8. JR radios have been available for some time in the U.S. from Circus Hobbies. I've gotten very good use out of two JR Century 7 systems. I use them in scale planes, where the mixing functions and dual rates come in handy. The Century 7 was one of the first FM systems available and is still one of the better ones.

JR has just introduced a computerized radio, the Galaxy Computer 8. It's an eight-channel system using PCM transmission, so it has the features that are common to PCM. It also has many if not most of the advanced features we've discussed in relation to other radios. What makes the Galaxy unique is that these features are turned on and off or adjusted with a one-line LCD readout rather than with switches and adjuster pots.

The Galaxy can be programmed with specific functions for seven different airplanes. You could control seven receivers with one Galaxy transmitter, each in a plane that required different functions. There are two Galaxy transmitters available, one for fixed-wing planes and one for helicopters, so one of your seven planes can't be a helicopter.

At the bottom of the Galaxy transmitter is a membrane-type sealed keypad and a readout. The readout uses liquid crystals (LCD) for display, so they show up well in bright sunlight out on the field. Using the keypad, you select the function you want and turn it on or off or adjust it.

The Pattern (fixed wing) Galaxy transmitter has reversing and travel adjustment on all channels, dual and exponential rates, flaperon differential, two preset snap roll functions, a V-tail mixer, a preset landing trim switch, and a servo test function. You can mix any two channels together. The Helicopter version gives you reversing and travel adjustment, a throttle hold switch, adjustable throttle curve, pitch curve adjustment, an invert switch, and acceleration gain control. Both radios incorporate a stop watch and an alarm timer.

JR radios are available direct from Circus Hobbies.

Multiplex. The famous German Multiplex radios are being imported by Beemer RC Service in Scottsdale, AZ. This is the radio I want to look at in detail, since I have plenty of experience with it. It's as sophisticated as they come. Incidentally, parts and service for this imported system are no problem. Beemer has their own technical facility on the premises, and can handle any and all repairs and tune-ups.

There are several Multiplex systems available. As with other European radios, they meet and exceed the 1991 frequency specifications; they've been operating under tighter specs in Europe for years. The most complex and most versatile unit in the Multiplex line is the Royal MC.

"MC" means "microcomputer." That's just what it is. Since it's a PCM system, there's a computer in the receiver, but the transmitter is also computer-controlled. One offshoot of this is that the Royal MC can control an FM receiver, too. This saves money; FM receivers are less expensive than PCM. It also means that if you don't want the slight but perceptible delay caused by a PCM receiver as it processes the incoming signal, you can switch to

The Multiplex Royal MC is one of the most advanced and versatile radio systems available. An interchangeable memory module will allow the radio to be used in any kind of model. You can store all switch and adjustor settings in its memory. It works with either FM or PCM receivers. (Photo by Jennifer Pratt)

FM. I like this for helicopters, where I want instant response; it's really a matter of taste, however.

The Multiplex PCM receiver incorporates several interesting features. It has a servo socket marked ''Z'' that performs a unique function. A servo connected to it sits at one end of its travel. When the receiver senses a low voltage level from its battery pack, the servo travels to the other end of its throw. You could use this to set off a light or a buzzer of some sort.

The receiver has a switch on the side that allows you to enable or disable fail-safe mode. Fail-safe means that if the receiver can't hear the transmitter any more, it moves all controls to a preset position. These positions are set at the factory as low throttle, all controls neutral, and a little bit of flaps. You can change these default positions by connecting a pushbutton switch to two terminals in one of the servo plugs, or you can switch out the fail-safe entirely. If you do this, the receiver will hold all controls in the position directed by the last clear signal.

Royal MC Transmitter. The Multiplex Royal MC transmitter is a marvel of versatility. It can be set up to offer specialized functions for helicopters, sport planes, V-tail planes, delta wings, aerobatic ships, competition sailplanes, flying wings, or boats. It does this with the Soft Module, an EPROM chip that snaps into the front of the system and changes its personality. There are 21 different Soft Modules.

All but a few of the switches on the transmitter are governed by the Soft Module. When you change Soft Modules, you also change the faceplate over the lower switches, and you can change the labels on the upper switches if it's necessary. The Soft Module can completely change the functions of the switches and adjuster pots. New Soft Modules are under development, so you can expect that your Multiplex transmitter will be upgradable to meet your future requirements.

Some Soft Modules incorporate a memory function. This means that you can record the settings of each switch and adjuster in the Soft Module. It will also record the trim positions. I use one of these modules when I fly my scale Shorts Skyvan, which uses a lot of the Multiplex radio's advanced mixing functions. I've programmed all of the functions I want for the Skyvan into the Soft Module's memory. When I set the memory switch to on, the stored positions override whatever position the switch is really in at the moment. When I move a trim lever, the transmitter beeps when it hits the position stored in the Soft Module. If I switch the memory off, all the switches and adjusters are returned to control. This allows me to fly two planes, each set up completely differently, with the same Soft Module.

The Multiplex transmitter with the appropriate Soft Module can offer you a huge range of features. Rudder and aileron can be mixed on one stick, and the amount of mixing is fully adjustable. You can also determine whether you want to add rudder with aileron, or aileron with rudder. Dual and exponential rates are available on all for primary channels: aileron, elevator, rudder, and throttle. Aileron differential is adjustable from the transmitter if you use a servo on each aileron; moving an adjuster gives you more up aileron than down or vice versa. Flaps can be mixed with ailerons, providing differential flap movement in a turn. Aileron can be mixed with flaps, giving you ailerons that droop when you drop the flaps. The elevator can be set to retrim itself when you drop the flaps, to compensate for changes in pitch. If you're using spoilers, elevator can be added automatically when they're deployed. You can set up the ailerons to act as flaps, drooping on command from another control while maintaining their differential throws. The extra channels can be controlled by two-position switches, three-position switches, or fully proportional slider controls. The end points of all these are adjustable.

With one of the four different Helicopter Soft Modules in place, you have more specialized functions. Collective pitch is mixed with throttle, of course. There is an adjustable throttle preselect point, also known as ''hovering throttle.'' Collective pitch is mixed with tail rotor speed. Gyro suppression is controllable from the transmitter during the flight. Flare compensation can be adjusted from the transmitter. Dual and exponential rates are available for pitch and roll. Autorotation controls for the throttle are switch-settable. Collective pitch can be trimmed separately.

Trims. When you move the trim switch on a standard transmitter, you move the servo off center. Suppose you add up trim to the elevator. The elevator will rest slightly up when the stick is centered. It'll also go up farther than it originally did when the stick is pulled all the way to maximum up. This doesn't happen on the Multiplex transmitter; the trims are only effective around neutral stick. So you can truly trim your airplane for hands-off flight, without changing the way it performs at the extremes of the control surface throw.

Throttle trim is slightly different. It only affects the end point of the throttle control. You can run the engine from low idle up to about half throttle with the trim alone, but when you move the throttle stick to full, you don't overdrive the servo.

Batteries. The receiver operates from the usual four-cell battery pack. Since PCM receivers are more sensitive to changes in voltage, a larger-than-normal pack is recommended if your plane has more than four servos in it. The standard pack has cells of 500 milliamp-hours (mAh) capacity. Packs with 800 and 1200 mAh cells are available. SR Batteries makes a pack that weighs almost the same as a standard 500 mAh pack, but is rated at 900 mAh. You should consider one of these with any PCM system.

The Multiplex transmitter is a bit of a departure. It operates from a six-cell pack instead of the American standard eight-cell pack. This means that the ordinary system charger won't work with the Multiplex. They sell a couple of chargers for it, but they're expensive. I use a Metered Vari-Charger from Ace RC, which automatically adjusts its output voltage to charge packs with from one to ten cells.

You can buy a second battery pack for the transmitter. A switch on top of the transmitter case controls which pack is powering the system. If one pack gets drained down to a low level, a loud beeper sounds. The beep changes to a steady tone when the condition is getting serious. You can switch over to the other pack instantly by moving the switch. The switch also allows you to charge both packs at once. You move the switch to the center position, connect your variable charger, and set it to deliver 100 mA of charge current. Circuitry within the battery switch distributes the charge current to the two packs, so that they each get the proper 50 mA of current for an overnight charge.

Prices. The Multiplex MC Royal system is available in several different configurations. You can start with the least expensive and buy expander modules to give you the top-of-the-line when you're ready. Upgrades include more channels, switched or on slider controls. A basic system, with an "All-round" Soft Module, PCM receiver, batteries, switches, and charge cables costs around $675. New Soft Modules will cost between $20 and $45, depending on the features you want. A PCM receiver costs around $174; the FM receiver that works with the Royal MC costs less than $134. Multiplex servos are priced between $30 and $74. Any positive pulse servo will work with the Multiplex receivers.

ELECTRONIC KITS

There are quite a few electronic kits on the market that will allow you to build useful equipment and save some money while you're at it. The largest electronic kit maker, Heathkit, no longer makes radio control systems; there are still some Heathkit sets in operation, though, which testifies to their quality.

Most of the electronic kits you'll see today come from Ace RC. All of Ace's kits are excellent; their instructions are clear and easy to follow, and the designs themselves are the best. They are clearly marked with a "skill level" so you have an idea about how much experience it takes to put one together. If you're intimidated by electronic construction, Ace's kits are available factory-assembled, but frankly, it's a lot of fun to build 'em yourself. I've built three Ace receivers, a Digipace battery cycler, several chargers, a Tachmaster tachometer, a Voltmaster meter, and a whole bunch of Ace servos. The only ones I had any trouble with were the servos, and that was because of their small size; once I got the hang of it I had no problems building more. One that I fatally fouled up was repaired quickly by Ace, so the lesson didn't even cost me that much.

Tools for Electronic Kits

You'll need a few specialized tools for building electronic kits. Your other tools—such as your knives, drill, pliers, tweezers, and occasionally even your sandpaper—will be useful.

A soldering iron is the most important tool. You don't need a very big or expensive one for electronic assembly; the important thing is that it should have a sharp tip. Most electronic kits in the RC field include integrated circuits ("chips"), and you have to get right up next to them with your soldering iron while not getting too much heat on the chip itself.

I have a cheap soldering iron that I use for most kit assembly; it's so old that I've had to file new points on the tip several times. It works fine for all but the most precise applications. I keep a damp piece of sponge handy to clean it as I work; it's important to keep the tip as clean as possible. Otherwise you run the risk of solder, dirt, and flux residue getting all over the circuit board and causing short circuits.

I've acquired a butane-powered soldering iron, and it's a real nice tool. It's about the size of a fat fountain pen. There's a spark wheel in the cap; you use it like a lighter to get the catalytic element in the solder head going. This element glows a bright red. There's no flame, so this iron is just as safe as a standard iron. It is up to operating temperature about 30 seconds after you light it. Of course, there's no cord to get tangled up in. And there's even a pocket clip on the iron cap. It sure comes in handy on the field when some solder joint lets go. I bought mine from Ace RC; they're available in hobby and electronics stores as well.

You'll need a good wire stripper. You can get along without one by using a sharp hobby knife to cut the insulation away from the wire. But it's tough, since you almost always cut into the wire. Ten bucks or so invested in a good wire stripper will more than pay for itself in saved time and frustration.

You'll also need a small pair of sharp diagonal cutters ("dikes"). They're very useful for cutting wires and clipping component leads close to the surface of the circuit board. Get a pair especially for electronic work, and don't use them to cut wire pushrods or landing gear!

The right solder is important. Use a brand that is specifically intended for electronics. I like to work

Using a liquid solder such as Supersafe and a holding fixture makes soldering connectors much easier. The soldering iron is butane-powered, with a catalytic element in the tip. (Photo by Jennifer Pratt)

with the smallest diameter solder wire I can find. Ace RC packages solder with their kits for you.

I also use a solder flux quite a lot. Supersafe liquid flux is the greatest thing going for "tinning" bare wires or contacts. Tinning is the process of flowing a bit of solder on the part that you will solder to something else. You should always tin bare wires; it makes them much easier to work with. You can do it with just an iron and wire solder, but the liquid flux makes it much easier. I keep the flux bottle sitting on the bench with a piece of thin tubing in it. I use the tubing to drop a drop of flux onto the end of the wire I want tinned. Then I put a drop of solder onto the tip of the iron. Touch it to the fluxed wire, and the solder immediately flows through all the wire strands. If I have a whole lot of wires to trim, I strip them all at once and clamp them in a "third hand," a little device that has a couple of clamps on adjustable arms attached to a heavy base. With five or six wires clamped in the third hand, it's quick work to flux and tin them all.

Electronic Assembly

The cardinal rule in building electronic kits is the same as any other kit: *Follow the instructions!* Assume that the people who designed the kit and wrote the instructions know more about this particular project than you do. That's the safest policy.

It's a lesson I've learned slowly, though. Only a few weeks ago I put together an Ace HD-500 charger kit. This is a single-output constant current charger designed to charge just about any battery pack, from a single cell to 12 cells and from 100 milliamps (mAh) to 4000 mAh. It's a simple kit, with a single circuit board, a transformer, and a meter. The board has a dozen or so resistors, two large capacitors, and a power transistor on it. I had it all soldered together in an hour, and assembled ready for testing in another hour. When I switched it on, the needle twitched . . . strange, since the other metered chargers I've built didn't do that. I plugged in a four-cell 1200 mAh pack. Whoa! The meter pegged to the high side, and the current knob didn't affect it. Unplug everything and check for proper polarity. Yes, it was fine. Off comes the case. I examined the insides very carefully, looking for stray wires, loose connections and shorts. Nothing obvious.

I reread the instructions. The only thing I hadn't done was to scrub the foil side of the completed circuit board with a toothbrush dipped in alcohol. This was supposed to be done after the board was completed, but I hadn't bothered. After all, the board looked pretty clean, and I'd gotten away without doing it in the past. But as I read the instructions again, I realized that this step was about all I could try . . . it was either a dirty circuit board causing my problem, or something was wrong with a component (rare but possible).

I plugged it in again. This time when I switched it on, the meter didn't twitch. I gingerly plugged in the battery pack—no problem. The charge current knob moved the meter just like it was supposed to. Hmmm. Was I sure I didn't have the pack plugged in backwards before? Then, as I watched, the charge current meter pegged itself to the right. Before I could get it unplugged, it had returned to where I had set it, then pegged again. All right, so I'm not hallucinating; there really *is* something wrong here.

I got an old toothbrush and some rubbing alcohol, and scrubbed down the foil side of the board. It was the simplest thing to try; I didn't even have to remove the board from its mount in the case. To make a long story short, the problem disappeared, and the charger hasn't done anything it shouldn't since. Lesson: Follow the instructions *exactly!*

Soldering

Ace kits include some nice instructions for the first-time kit builder. They spend a good deal of time talking about proper soldering technique, since this is one place where a lot of beginners make mistakes.

There are a few rules for good soldering. The first one is to use enough heat. This is largely a matter of patience: Don't shove the solder against the iron to melt it. Put the iron against the point to be soldered, and have the patience to hold it there until you can melt the solder by touching it to the part, not the iron. This is the way to avoid "cold" solder joints that are brittle and can loosen with vibration.

Another rule is to keep the tip of your iron clean. An old sponge with a little water in it will give you a good spot to wipe the iron tip. This will keep it free of charred flux and melted insulation.

Finally, keep safety in mind while you're at this work. Keep the cord of the iron away from your feet. If you push back your chair and knock the iron off the table, you could burn yourself or start a fire. Don't leave hot irons unattended.

Kit Radios

As I mentioned earlier, Heathkit used to produce a kit that built into an RC system. Unfortunately, some years ago they decided to get out of the RC business. The only other kit-built radio systems are sold by Ace RC.

The Silver Seven radio system was produced on Ace RC's 25th anniversary a few years ago, and in the intervening time has built up a reputation as one of the finest systems on the market.

The Silver Seven transmitter has a plug-in RF deck, meaning that the circuitry that determines the frequency you're operating on is interchangeable. You can get RF decks from Ace for any of the RC bands, so your Silver Seven transmitter can be used to operate any kind of model. This is especially useful for scale boat modelers, who often need more than the three channel radios that are usually available on surface model frequencies. Remember, it's against federal law to operate out-of-band; if you have a radio on a frequency in the aircraft band, it's illegal to use it in a car or a boat! Silver Seven RF decks are also available in the 27 mHz band, which is unregulated.

One of the features I like best about the Silver Seven is the fact that you can put the switches and buttons where they're most comfortable for you. Many fliers prefer to have the trim switches that adjust the elevator and ailerons over on the left (throttle) stick, where they don't have to let go of the right stick to adjust them. This is called "crossed trims." You can easily build in this feature as you build the transmitter.

You can even customize your system further with a Silver Seven option called the "Experimenter's Kit." It's a standard Silver Seven transmitter kit, but no holes have been drilled in the transmitter case. You can put the sticks, switches, and buttons anywhere on the box you happen to want them. If you fly single-stick, you can mount the stick at an angle that you find most comfortable with the way you cradle the box in your left hand.

The Silver Seven receiver is one of the best available in terms of noise and interference rejection. Since it's made in the U.S. by a relatively small company, it's been continually upgraded in response to the market. It is presently available only in an AM version, but can be tuned to any RC frequency in all three bands.

At the time of this writing, Ace was showing a new receiver that meets (and exceeds) the 1991 frequency standards. This "Model 91" receiver will be on the market by the time you read this, and will retail for under $100 factory-assembled. The kit version will cost less, of course. This could become the "standard" add-on receiver for transmitters of just about any brand that have been approved to operate in 1991.

Chapter 3

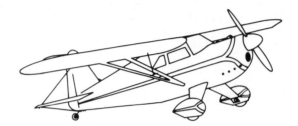

Specialized Planes

THIS CHAPTER IS HOME FOR DISCUSSION OF SEV-
eral kinds of airplanes that don't fit neatly into
other categories. They are all items that sport fliers
are interested in, and you're very likely to see them
at the average flying field.

Some of the planes we're going to discuss are
intended for competition. What's this doing in a book
for sport fliers? Well, the fact is that the great
majority of competition plane kits that are sold never
wind up in competition; the people who own them
get their pleasure out of flying them at their own
speed and on their own time. Apparently, the average modeler likes to hone his flying skills on competition airplanes, whether he actually flies them in
competition or not.

We'll also use this chapter to cover a lot of aircraft designs that are not for beginners, but not
oriented toward a specific competition.

AEROBATICS

To many sport fliers, the measure of a performance plane is its ability to "fly the Pattern," or
perform a series of specific maneuvers. Most of
these maneuvers are excellent for improving your
piloting skills. Maybe you can't complete the whole
Pattern schedule of maneuvers in one flight, but your
Pattern plane is capable of it and will help you learn.

There are many different aircraft you can select for sport pattern flying. I favor models that are
scale or semi-scale representations of full-size aerobatic aircraft. The CAP-21, Laser 200, and Pitts
Special come to mind right away. Great Planes
Manufacturing makes a whole series of CAP kits for
different engine sizes. The SIG Pitts is a classic; if
you want something larger and fancier, there's the
famous Quarter Scale Pitts from Byron Originals.

If you like, there are plenty of almost-ready-to-
fly planes with aerobatic capability. Zimpro Marketing is importing a series of gorgeous ARFs that are
made in Zimbabwe. They come with the fuselages
completely assembled. The wings are foam cores,
sheeted with thin wood. Finish them the way you
like and install your own radio and engine. You can
also order several Zimpro kits completely finished
and painted.

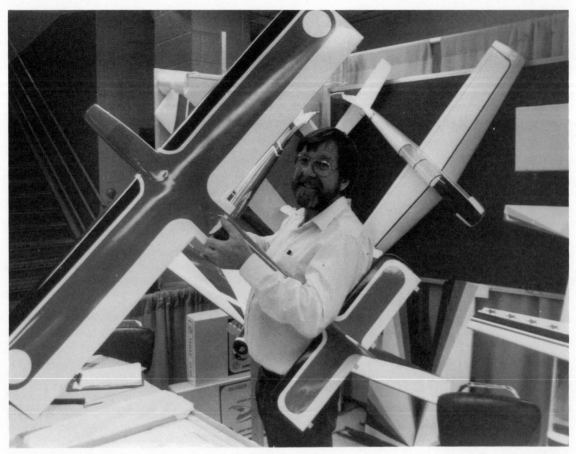

Zimbabwe Model Products produces beautiful handmade models at their factory in Africa; they're sold in the United States by Zimpro Marketing. Here, Dennis Hunt of Zimpro shows off one of their sport aerobatic planes. You can get them built, or covered and finished to your order. (Photo by Holly English Payne)

Sticks. Sooner or later, at every flying field, you'll see someone flying a variation of the "Ugly Stick." The basic Stick is instantly recognizable: a long fuselage ending in a flat firewall and an engine out in the open, a big wide wing, and a round vertical tail. You'll see 'em in all sizes and colors.

Stick kits are available from several different manufacturers. The most popular are the "Sweet Stick" series from Midwest Products. There are several sizes of Sweet Sticks, including a biplane and a "Sweet and Low Stick" with the wing on the bottom of the fuselage instead of the top. You can also buy almost-ready-to-fly Stick models from Indy RC and World Engines.

Since the engine is out in the open, Stick models will accept a large variety of powerplants. Most of the ones I've seen around are grossly overpowered, but that seems to be what people prefer. I have a Super Sweet Stick that I use for testing engines from two-stroke .40s to four-stroke 1.20s. By using an Edson adjustable motor mount, I can mount almost all of the engines I've used in this size range without changing mounts as well.

Airtronics Jetfire. Airtronics sells several kits that will appeal to the Sport Pattern flier. Airtronics kits are exceptional. All of the shaped wood parts are precut and sanded; the ribs are band-sawn rather than die-cut. All hardware is included; all you need to add is a tank and wheels. The instructions are photo-illustrated every step of the way. Full-size

"Stick" is a family name for a group of similar sport planes. They have boxy fuselages, wide wings, and round vertical fins. This is a Sweet Stick .40 from Midwest Products. Midwest sells several sizes of Sweet Sticks, including a biplane and a low-wing. (Photo courtesy *Model Retailer* magazine)

plans include a lot of helpful information. Airtronics kits are an outstanding value for the sport flier.

I've enjoyed flying the Airtronics Jetfire .40, a shoulder-wing sport aerobatics airplane. Thanks to the quality of the parts, it was easy to assemble; in fact, I built the wing during a demonstration of model building at the National Air and Space Museum. The nose section is built up from thick balsa sheet and shaped to conform to whatever engine you want to mount. A balsa block on top of the forward section of the fuselage allows you to make a smooth transition up to the leading edge of the wing. It gives you a racy-looking plane!

Wing construction isn't unusual. Since most parts are preshaped, it goes together easily. There's only ¾ inch of dihedral in the wing, so it's simple to join the wing halves by blocking one wingtip up 1½ inches. The tips are carved and shaped from square blocks. The ailerons run the full length of the trailing edge. I used D-Hinges to attach the ailerons, removing a ⅛ inch strip from the leading edge of each aileron to fill in between the D-Hinges (see Chapter 4 of *The Beginner's Guide to Radio Control Sport Flying*, TAB Book No. 3020, for a complete description of these hinges).

I decided to make the Jetfire a taildragger. I simply moved the landing gear forward until the axles were parallel with the wing leading edge. I moved the plywood doubler in the bottom of the fuselage forward as well, so the landing gear would bolt into the plywood.

I covered the Jetfire with black MonoKote. This is the classic covering material, and it works extremely well for almost all models. Covering the Jetfire's smooth curves was easy. I sealed the edges of the MonoKote around the engine compartment with thin CyA glue. This keeps engine oil from working its way back in underneath the MonoKote and loosening its grip. I trimmed the Jetfire with white striping tape purchased at an auto supply store; it gave me a neat double pinstripe. I wasn't certain that the automotive tape would stand up to hot engine exhaust, so I shot a light coat of Black Baron Clear spray epoxy over it.

The Jetfire has flown with an Enya Sport .40 two-stroke and an HP .49 four-stroke engine. The HPs are out of production, but there are still plenty of them around. On the whole, I got better performance with the Enya. The HP allowed me to use a large three-bladed prop, a Zinger 10-7. This gave

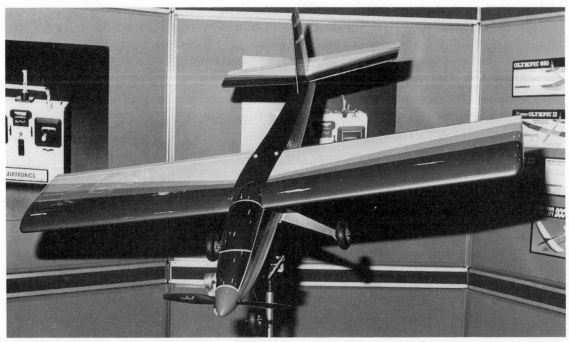

The Airtronics Jetfire .40 is a smooth, sleek aerobatic airplane. It can be powered by any modern .40 two-stroke. Airtronics kits are very complete, and feature beautiful hand-cut parts. (Photo courtesy of *Model Retailer* magazine)

pleasing vertical performance, and slowed the plane down in maneuvers. With full throttle on the Enya, the Jetfire was a real guided missile!

Thanks to its relatively large semi-symmetrical wing, the Jetfire will fly at a very wide range of speeds. When you set it up on final approach, you can reduce the throttle to idle and add up elevator to keep the plane level. It'll slow up nicely, and you'll

The SIG Kobra is one of the most popular sport aerobatics planes around. With a .40 engine, it'll do every maneuver in the book. SIG sells decal sets for several different color schemes. (Photo courtesy SIG Manufacturing)

find that you have solid aileron control despite the low speed and nose-up attitude. This makes the Jet-fire very easy to land. From the first flight, I've had no trouble dropping it in for three-point landings, touching both wheels and the tailskid at the same moment.

Ace RC's Four-Stroke Squadron. Ace RC has released a whole series of performance planes designed for sport aerobatic flying. They started with a design called the 4-40; the name meant that the plane was intended for four-stroke .40 size engines. It worked so well that Ace followed it up with a 4-60 and a 4-20. They worked, too. Now Ace has a 4-120, a 4-40 biplane, and a 4-120 bipe on the way. Ace's approach to kit design seems to me to be similar to that of people who plan TV programs: If something works once, beat it to death.

I picked the 4-60 as a good example of what the Stroker Squadron is all about. One thing that impressed me immediately was the amount of hardware included in the kit. You'll need wheels, an engine mount, and a fuel tank; everything else is there.

The 4-60 kit doesn't have a full-size fuselage drawing. It isn't really needed—the half-size sketch shows how the cut fuselage parts fit, and that's all you need. The pieces are keyed together so you can't misalign them.

I got the 4-60 fuselage assembled in record time. The fuselage was framed, stringers installed on the turtledeck, engine mount and firewall installed, and landing gear mounted in three hours and 15 minutes. I didn't hurry either, taking the time to smooth the edges of the light ply die-cut pieces with a sanding block. The parts fit was excellent; the fuselage is virtually self-jigging.

I removed the choke lever from the Enya .60 to simplify the engine installation. It would have required a hole out the side of the fuselage. I've found that it's very easy to flood an engine that has a flap-type choke. I generally use an electric starter on four-strokes when they're dry, after a few hand flips to make certain they really *are* dry. Flooded engines are more likely to backfire, run backwards, or kick a prop loose.

There isn't a drop of epoxy in the fuselage of

Ace RC has produced a whole range of kits just for sport aerobatics with four-stroke engines. Above are the 4-40 (left) and the 4-60, for .40 and .60 engines respectively. They're smooth, solid fliers. (Photo by Jennifer Pratt)

my 4-60, thanks to Slow Jet. I found that Slow Jet works beautifully for installing the firewall, since it doesn't run. I attached the firewall with plenty of Slow Jet; the fuselage sides fit perfectly, so no clamping was necessary. Super Jet was used for reinforcing and attaching the triangle strips behind the firewall. Finally, I used Instant Jet to fuelproof the firewall and front of the fuselage. The only caveat here is not to get too close to this or any other super glue when it goes off! The gas it produces can take your breath away for a few seconds.

I looked all over for the bottom piece of the engine compartment, then looked at the plans and discovered there isn't one. So much for conventional wisdom.

I used a Tatone engine mount for my Enya .60, which has long arms and is a little wider than the same size Hayes mount. This meant that I had to rout a couple of slots in the inner surfaces of the nose side pieces, so they would come together behind the spinner in front. This was easy, but I'm glad I test-fitted it before I glued the sides on!

The nose piece that fits behind the spinner needs to be trimmed with a razor saw to fit, depending on how much taper you put in the two side pieces. I cut a semicircle in the top of this piece and fitted it up around the engine to give me a little more strength in the nose.

Shaping the three nose pieces is made a lot easier by using some really coarse sandpaper. My Wedge Lock block allows easy changing to any grit I have handy. I worked out the basic shape with a coarse belt, then went to 400 grit to smooth it out.

I found the wing very simple to build. It's assembled in two pieces with a dihedral brace, like most sportplane wings. One difference is the spruce strips that go around the curved part of the top leading edge. These "turbulator strips" serve to break up the surface airflow coming over the front of the wing, which helps it move more smoothly over the wing. It's like the dimples in a golf ball.

I used epoxy to glue the two wing halves together, to give me time to prop up one wingtip at the proper angle. The kit includes a strip of cloth to reinforce the joint between the wings. I attached this strip starting under the leading edge of the wing

with a bead of Super Jet. I smoothed the cloth down over the Super Jet and gave it a shot of accelerator. Then I worked it up and over the leading edge, across the top, and around the trailing edge, spreading a little Super Jet ahead of the cloth to stick it down. Once it was all down, I gave it a coat of Slow Jet, spread across and into the cloth with a strip of plastic. It set up smooth and fast, and as strong as epoxy.

The wing is held on by two nylon bolts. I like this system, since it's a lot neater than rubber bands. You fit two hardwood blocks under the wing saddle area of the fuselage on the inside edges. The wing rests flat on these blocks. You drill through the wing into the blocks. Then you widen the holes in the wing to clear the nylon bolts, and tap the holes in the blocks. Ace sells a set of taps that will thread these holes neatly; they come with a T-bar handle. You could also use a wing mounting kit from Wing Manufacturing, available at your hobby shop. The Wing Mfg. kit includes nylon bolts, and brass insets that have coarse threads on the outside and threads that fit the nylon bolts on the inside. You drill your holes, then screw the brass inserts into the holes in the blocks. This is an excellent system, since you won't have any problem with the threads in the brass inserts.

For a final touch, after the 4-60 is covered, you add a windshield on top of the wing and a pilot bust. What better pilot then Ace's Cap'n Eddy? The Cap'n is molded in flexible, flesh-colored plastic that accepts almost any kind of paint; you can even buy him prepainted. I don't generally put pilot busts in my planes, since I'm not crazy about little dolls staring woodenly ahead, but Cap'n Eddy has character.

Radio installation is simple. I used an Airtronics sport system, which is in my experience one of the best everyday radios you can get.

When I took the 4-60 out to the field the first time, the engine was new and I wanted to get some running on it before flying it. I ran two tanks through the Enya .60 with the plane tied down and the needle valve set rich, gradually leaning it out. On the third tank, the engine was running so smoothly I decided to let 'er rip. I set it safely rich and taxied out to the runway.

The Super Demon is a hot little sport plane from Scande Research. It's capable of all the aerobatic maneuvers. Instead of using elevons and mixing elevator and aileron electronically, the Demon models use separate elevators and ailerons. This means ordinary radio systems will work very well in these models. (Photo courtesy *Model Retailer* magazine)

The 4-60 pointed itself into the wind and took of before I had the throttle more than two-thirds open. Two clicks of down elevator trim and I was flying as solidly as if the plane was an old friend. I made several circuits to listen to the engine, then tried some rolls. For a plane with such a large wing, the roll rate is remarkable; I can get in three axial rolls in the length of the field. Finally, I gave it full throttle and tried some inverted flight. It held inverted with just a bit of forward stick, and handled as nicely as could be. The engine got rich after a few minutes of inverted flight, and just as I was beginning to get concerned about it, it quit.

So there I was, about 80 feet in the air, upside down, dead stick. Explaining my next maneuver without showing it to you is difficult, but suffice it to say I executed an abrupt and sloppy snap roll by slamming the sticks to the bottom left corner of the transmitter. The 4-60 flipped wheels down immediately, leaving me to concentrate on recovering enough airspeed to reach the field. That's when I got my next surprise: The 4-60 glides better than anything I've flown that wasn't a sailplane or an Old-Timer with a long wing. I got back with runway to spare.

The 4-60 has turned into my proficiency plane. I practice maneuvers with it; it'll do anything in the book. The nicest part is the fact that it does the maneuvers slowly enough that I can think them through. I've become a better pilot from flying the plane—and enjoyed it, besides.

Lanier Jester. Lanier RC produces a wide range of kits that are largely prefabricated. Most of them have wings with a semi-symmetrical airfoil, giving them excellent aerobatic capability. I've been flying the Lanier Jester, one of their more popular planes.

The Jester, like other Lanier kits, comes with a ready-made fuselage. The fuselage is a wooden crutch with molded plastic sides bonded to it. You cut the plastic away from the engine compartment to clear whatever engine you want to use. When you do, you find two hardwood rails in the right position to be engine mounts. You can fit a wide range of engines in there. I recommend a powerful .40 or .60 for the Jester; it flies fast. Bubba Spivey of Lanier flies his Jester with a piped RJL .60; he likes guided missiles. I settled for a Rossi .40, which has more than enough power with the stock muffler.

Lanier wings and tail surfaces are covered with a sheet plastic material that will shrink with the application of heat. You don't want to warm it with an iron, though; that's too much heat in too small an area. Use a hair dryer or heat gun. It's a good idea to shrink the plastic covering the elevator, ailerons, and rudder before gluing the hinges in place, especially at the ends. When you have a good fit, you install the hinges and control horns the same way you do with any other plane.

Opening up the fuselage in the wing mount area exposes the internal rails where you mount the servos. First, though, you should put in the fuel tank. This fits behind the engine compartment. Put it in place, then drill the bulkhead that fits in front of it to clear the fuel lines. Glue this bulkhead in place with the fuel lines going into the engine compartment. Now you can fuelproof the engine compartment with epoxy. My favorite way of doing this is to mix a batch of epoxy and thin it with a little rubbing alcohol until it flows. You can pour it in and flow it around the whole compartment, letting the excess run back into your mixing cup. Thinning the epoxy doesn't affect its curing time. Another alternative is using Pic Coating Poxy, which is thin enough as it comes out of the bottle to be brushed right into the compartment.

Lanier kits include special solvent-type glue to use on the sheet plastic. Use this to fit the tail surfaces into the fuselage, after opening up slots in the recesses provided. CyA glues will stick to the plas-

Lanier RC makes a line of almost-ready-to-fly models for sport and aerobatic flying. They are very strong! This is the Lanier Laser, a semi-scale model of the famous Laser aerobatic plane. It's designed for large four-stroke engines. (Photo courtesy Lanier RC)

tic, but epoxy doesn't hold as well unless you sand the surface to roughen it. You don't want to do this on any area that shows, so use the supplied glue.

Once the tail surfaces are in place, install your pushrods. I like to use Sullivan flexible rods; in the Jester I used the large semi-rigid rods, since the control runs are nice and straight. Roughen the outer tube of the rod with sandpaper so glue will stick to it better.

Joining the wing halves is straightforward. Measure them to be sure that you get the correct dihedral angle; it may be necessary to trim away a little foam from the mating surfaces with a knife. Use lots of epoxy, wiping away the excess that oozes out of the joint. When this is set, glue the preformed joint coverings in place with the plastic cement provided.

The ailerons use torque rods for control. It's easy to install these under a plastic doubler at the rear of the wing center section. The ailerons fit down over them, and the servo connects to the projecting rod ends. I used Goldberg aileron horn sets for mine; they include servo connections that can be screwed up and down the rod ends to change the amount of aileron throw. I cut a hole in the center of the wings to install the servo. I screwed the servo to small hardwood rails, inserted it into the hole until the rails touched the surface of the wing, and glued the rails down with epoxy.

I used self-adhesive Trim MonoKote to finish the Jester wing; if you use an iron-on, make sure your iron temperature is low. It didn't take long to turn out the model, and it's a hot flying machine. The construction is fairly heavy, but boy, is it tough; a Lanier plane will take just about any punishment a plane will get. This is the plane to practice on and get your courage up to trying new maneuvers.

OLD-TIMERS

There is a curious category of model airplanes commonly known as "Old-Timers." It's a pretty flexible term, but it generally refers to airplanes that were designed before the 1960s. The Society of Antique Modelers (SAM) has created a list of designs that fall into Antique, Vintage, and Old-Timer categories for the purposes of the competitions they run. SAM competition is very low-key; it consists mostly

of admiring each others' airplanes. Delightful stuff.

Old-Timer planes are distinguished by large wings, light wing loadings, and the ability to fly without help from radio control. When these planes were designed, radio control was either nonexistent or very tenuous. As a result, when you modernize one of these designs by adding a throttle, a rudder, and an elevator, you get a very easy airplane to fly. This is one of the reasons for the strong, growing interest in Old-Timers.

Electric power is very suitable to Old-Timer planes. Their large wings will generally handle the extra weight of the battery packs easily. Since many of the engines available in the 1930s and '40s weren't as powerful as the ones we use today, the lower power output of electric flight systems fits these designs well. The most obvious example of this is the Senior Playboy kit made by Leisure Electronics for their geared motor system. Old-Timer kits designed for electric motors are also made by Astro Flight. Many Old-Timer kits can easily be modified for electric power; a friend of mine put an Astro Flight 05 Cobalt geared motor in a Miss America kit from Hobby Horn, with excellent results. See Chapter 1 for more information about electric flight.

You can expect Old-Timer designs to be more complicated to build than more modern kits. Modern kits often have fuselages that are built from solid sheet sides; building them is a matter of attaching the sides squarely to fuselage formers. Old-Timer fuselages are usually built with sticks, cut to shape and glued down over a plan, and joined with crosspieces. This takes longer and requires more effort, but produces a much lighter structure than the modern method. For a complete description of how to build like this, look at out discussion of Schoolyard Scale models in Chapter 5.

Several magazines periodically publish Old-Timer plans. *Model Builder* magazine is in the vanguard of the Old-Timer movement, with several Old-Timer articles each month. They carry John Pond's excellent "Plug Sparks" column, which is the best source for pictures and information on what other Old-Timer modelers are building. You'll frequently find plans and drawings of famous and obscure Old-Timer designs, with brief histories, in *Model*

This lovely Old Timer-style model was built by Roger Taylor of the San Diego Aeroneers club. It uses an Astro Cobalt 05 electric motor system for power. (Photo courtesy *Model Aviation* magazine)

Builder. You can buy *Model Builder* at your hobby shop; to subscribe, write to them at the address found in Appendix B.

Old-Timer Sources

Because of the strong interest in Old-Timers, a lot of plans have been reprinted. Most of the model magazines have dozens of Old-Timers in their plan lists. Cleveland Model and Supply Company has a huge assortment of plans, many from their famous kits of the 1930s and '40s. Their catalog costs $2. John Pond's Old-Timer Plans Service is another excellent source; John has all of the classics.

Several companies sell Old-Timer kits. Hobby Horn is one of the best sources. They carry the P&W line of kits, which have machine-cut parts, all the strip wood necessary, and the original Free Flight-style plans. Any of the kits is easily converted

to RC by adding a rudder to the fin and an elevator to the stabilizer. Hobby Horn also has the fine Midway kits, including the Buzzard Bombshell, Flying Quaker, and Dennyplane Jr. $2 brings their catalog.

Champion Model Aeroplane Company kits Sal Taibi's famous Powerhouse. This classic design is perfect for a .60 four-stroke engine. The Champion kit is a very close reproduction, modified from the 1939 Powerhouse only enough to accommodate three channels of RC.

Antique Engines

Thanks to the tremendous interest in Old-Timers, several suppliers of antique engines have appeared. Micro Model Engineering makes parts for antique engines that will turn old ''junkers'' into ''runners.'' They have over 600 items in their catalog; it costs $2. T&D Research is producing a replica

SIG's Astro Hog is a modern version of one of the first planes designed for radio control aerobatics. With a modern four-stroke engine, it can do all the maneuvers in the book—slowly enough for the sport flier to keep up with it. (Photo courtesy SIG Manufacturing)

The Christen Eagle is a famous aerobatic biplane; several model companies sell kits of the Eagle. This one is from Indy RC, and comes already built and painted, requiring a few hours of assembly. (Photo courtesy *Model Retailer* magazine)

of the Edco Sky Devil ignition engine. I've seen these at trade shows, and they are beautiful pieces of metalwork. Super Cyclone Engines has several reproductions of the famous old Super Cykes in production. Each engine is tested at the factory, and they come with coil, condenser, and spark plug.

The best source of information on antique engines is the Model Engine Collectors Association (MECA). They publish a newsletter, and hold regular Collectogethers at trade shows, contests, and the AMA NATS. You can get MECA's current address from Appendix G.

Chapter 4

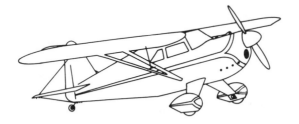

Soaring

RADIO-CONTROLLED SOARING IS A FACET OF THE hobby that has pleasures all its own. For one thing, it can be very simple. You don't have to fool around with engines; you learn the ways of winds and air currents instead. Most common sailplanes are easier to learn to fly than powered planes, because they move more slowly through the air. A beginner can stay ahead of a sailplane more easily and plan what he wants the plane to do, rather than reacting to it.

HOW DO THEY STAY UP?

Once it comes off the launch line, a typical sailplane will take a couple of minutes to come back to the ground, even in the hands of a rank beginner. So how do they stay up for as long as half an hour? The trick is to spot *thermal currents*, rising vortices of warm air.

A thermal can be thought of as a moving fountain of air. (A friend of mine once observed, "After all, water is just fat air.") This fountain rises up from warm patches of ground as the sun warms the sur-

face of the planet. Thermals can be tiny gusts that push a couple of leaves, or they can be trash-movers a quarter mile or more in diameter.

Like a fountain, the warm air rises up through the middle of the circle. Cold air is moving downward along the edges of the column of rising air, like water cascading down from a fountain. This cold air can bring you down faster than the thermal keeps you up! So the trick is to turn smoothly within the rising warm air, avoiding the "down air" at the edges of the thermal column.

It's easier than it sounds. Most sailplanes have wings that will support the plane easily through very tight turns. In fact, you can often stand the plane right on its wingtip and pirouette for a couple of turns by holding up elevator, then come smoothly out of the turn by releasing elevator and gently adding rudder in the opposite direction.

When you notice a thermal, your next step is to measure it. Turn and move until the moving air rocks the wings again. Keep turning until you get an idea of where the borders of the thermal are. Then you can make wide, flat turns within the ther-

The Robbe RC-Start is a beginner's sailplane. It's largely prefabricated, with a molded hi-impact plastic fuselage and sheeted foam wings. The tail is removable for easy transportation. (Photo courtesy Robbe USA)

mal, exposing as much of your wing as possible to the rising air.

WING GEOMETRY

One feature that gives a plane the ability to turn so tightly is the *dihedral angle* of the wing, the angle at which the wingtips are swept upward, making the wing panels form a "V" when viewed from the front. On powered planes you're probably familiar with dihedral angles of two degrees or so. Some sailplanes (as well as Free Flight and Old-Timer airplanes) have a dihedral angle of five degrees or greater. If the wing is made up of four panels, each of which is set at an angle, the wing has *polyhedral*. A polyhedral wing generally has more of the good characteristics of a wing with simple dihedral.

Dihedral and Polyhedral

Dihedral and polyhedral give a certain amount of automatic stability. As the plane banks, the wing that is going up produces less lift, and must move faster to maintain lift. That's what pulls the plane through a turn. Conversely, the lower wing produces more lift. If the wings are set at a high angle of dihedral, the lower wing's tendency to produce more

lift will try to rock the plane back in the opposite direction of bank. As it does this, the lower wing loses lift and the higher wing gains some. So the bank becomes self-correcting, and the plane will tend to fly level.

Washout

Another trick of airplane design that enhances this self-correcting effect is called *washout*. It refers to the angle of the wingtips. Visualize the centerline of the aircraft from nose to tail, then look at the plane sideways, and draw an imaginary line on the wingtip from the leading edge to the trailing edge. Washout is the angle at which this line is higher at the trailing edge than at the leading edge. The opposite effect, *wash-in*, is obtained when the wingtip is swept down at the trailing edge. Wash-in is rarely used, since it can have a turning effect; you see it occasionally in Free Flight models, which are designed to turn.

Washout is your most effective weapon against tip stall. *Tip stall* is the tendency of the tip of the wing to lose lift, or stall, in tight turns. As the lower wing drops in a tight turn, the air flowing over it slows and it loses lift. If the air slows past the stalling speed of the wing, the plane abruptly drops its wingtip. This can often lead to an unplanned snap roll. Washout counteracts this tendency by presenting a better angle of attack as the wing drops. So if the inward panel of the wing loses lift, the tip is still lifting and can hold it in position. Washout helps you maintain solid control in a turn.

Some airplane kits tell you to add washout to the wing during construction. When the plans show a wingtip where the last three or four ribs are angled slightly upward at the trailing edge, you're building in washout. The same effect can be achieved by ribs that are shaped differently, curving upward more at the bottom and flattening out on the top toward the trailing edge. If your plane has ailerons, you can get the effect of washout by *reflexing* the ailerons; that is, adjusting the aileron connectors so that both ailerons are slightly up at neutral. But the most common sailplanes don't have ailerons, so you'll have to add washout other ways.

Truing the Wing

You can usually add washout to a wing easily after it's covered. This is done when you "true" the wing. Truing the wing is the process of removing any warps that may have been built into the wing structure. You do it after covering the wing, if you're using an iron-on covering. A sheeted foam wing won't require it, since you couldn't build a warp into a foam wing if you wanted to.

Set your covering iron at the temperature recommended for shrinking the covering you used on the wing. Now lay the wing, a panel at a time, flat on your building board. The center panels should be flat on the board, viewed from the front and back. Look at the edges of the panel to see if the leading or trailing edge of the panel is twisted upward. If you see a twist, you'll have to use the covering material to take it out.

Secure the panel to the building board so that all four corners are flat. This can be done with pins

The SR-7 from Bob Martin RC Models is a hot, fast slope-soaring machine. It uses two channels of RC: ailerons and elevator. Bob Martin makes a wide range of sailplane kits, as well as a few gas-powered planes. (Photo courtesy *Model Retailer* magazine)

angled into the board (not stuck through the wing!) or with small weights. Sandbags are useful for this; I have a set of small bags sold by Bell Rock Industries that I filled with lead shot. Run your covering iron over the entire surface of the panel. This will reshrink the covering into a position that will help hold the wing flat. Let it cool, remove the weights or pins, and inspect the wing. This is often all it takes to fix a wing warp.

If your inspection shows that the warp is still there, try supporting the wing upside down and heating the covering on the underside of the wing.

If you still have a wing warp, you can try one more trick. Pick up the wing and twist it in the opposite direction from the warp. Then hold it about two feet over an electric stove burner set to high. Move it around: don't hold it in one place over the burner. Do this for no more than 20 seconds, then move the wing away from the heat and hold it in position while it cools. Reinspect the wing. You could have just put in a warp in the opposite direction!

Any of these techniques will work to add the washout you want to the wingtips. Set up the wing on your building board with a block under the trailing edge wingtip that puts it at the proper washout angle. Run your iron over the covering, let it cool, remove the wing from the building board, and inspect.

SAILPLANE TYPES

Sailplanes tend to fall into distinct categories, based on the competition classes they fit into. *Hand-launched* sailplanes have wingspans of 1 ½ meters or less. These have become very popular in the last year or so. Most require miniature receivers and servos. Most common are the *Two-Meter* sailplanes, with wingspans of two meters or slightly less. They're a convenient size for sport fliers and are friendly to fly. *Standard* class sailplanes have wingspans of more than two meters, up to 100 inches. These are common among serious soaring enthusiasts. *Unlimited* sailplanes have wingspans over 100 inches; these huge beauties are seldom seen except at contests. *Scale* sailplanes have a hard core of admirers, but are also relatively rare except at contests. *F3B* ships are designed expressly for

the international class of competition; they must be able to travel at high speeds as well as achieve a certain flight time.

SAILPLANE KITS

There are many fine sailplane kits on the market. If soaring appeals to you, you'll have no trouble getting into it.

The Gentle Lady from Carl Goldberg Models is a Two-Meter sailplane that has become very popular. People like its ease of construction. It's a sweet-flying airplane that a rank beginner can handle.

Top Flite Models has produced several interesting sailplanes designed by noted soaring competitor Scott Christensen. The Metrick is a two-meter ship that will hold its own in competition, and is still simple and easy to fly. The Wristocrat is a neat little Hand-Launched ship that can be competitive at contests, but really shines on a sunny afternoon's fun flying. The Wristocrat kit includes a solid balsa replica of the model for one of the smaller members of your family to build and fly while you're building and flying yours.

Airtronics has several classic sailplanes designed by Lee Renaud. They're classics because they're hard to improve on. The Olympic II (Standard class) and Olympic 650 (Two-Meter) are flown a lot at contests. Like other Airtronics kits, the quality is outstanding and all necessary hardware is included.

Davey Systems sells several very nice sailplane kits. The famous Prophet is available in Two-Meter and Standard sizes. A second plan sheet in each kit shows optional wing configurations and suggestions for installing an electric motor. Their newest kit is the Ariel, a little 1 ½ meter ship that's light enough to hand launch.

Robbe sells several sailplane kits. They're best known for their Scale ships, most notably their ASW-19. Like most Robbe kits, the fuselages are molded from high-impact plastic. The wings are foam cores that come sheeted with light veneer. This prefabrication does the most tedious assembly for you, and almost guarantees a ship that is straight and true. Robbe kits are only available through hobby shops.

The magnificent Airtronics Olympic II has been a popular Standard class sailplane for many years. The two-piece wing disassembles for easier transportation. Airtronics kits are very complete, giving you all the hardware you need. (Photo courtesy Airtronics, Inc)

LAUNCHING SAILPLANES

There are several different methods of getting sailplanes in the air. Whatever method is used, the purpose is the same: Give the ship enough momentum to reach an altitude where it can take advantage of rising air. Smaller sailplanes can be launched by hand. A light toss will get them in the air, and they are usually light enough to take advantage of weak thermals and wind currents that are close to the ground. Many hand-launched sailplanes are reinforced to take a much stronger throw; they can be thrown sidearm at high speed and zoom up to 100 feet.

Most sailplanes use one of two devices for launching: a *winch*, or a *hi-start*. A hi-start consists of about 100 feet of surgical rubber tubing, usually 3/16 inch in diameter, with another 400 feet of strong fishing line tied to it. The rubber is staked into the ground on the downwind side of the field. The tubing and line are laid out in the same direction that the wind is blowing. A parachute and a ring are attached to the line. The whole business is stretched out another 100 to 200 feet, until there is sufficient pull from the stretched tubing. The plane hooks onto the ring in the parachute.

Holding the plane firmly in your right hand and your transmitter in your left, point the nose of the plane at the horizon and release it in a smooth motion. It will zoom up as the tubing contracts. Near the top of the launch, your plane will be gaining altitude on its own and will start to pull the tubing back out again. At maximum altitude, a quick touch of down elevator will slip the plane off the ring. The parachute snaps open and the line returns to the ground while you start looking for rising air.

On the way up, you should be concentrating on keeping the plane traveling in a straight line. Some fliers like to give the plane a little down elevator during the first few seconds of the launch to help it build up speed and stretch the rubber out more at the top.

Hi-starts are inexpensive, easy to carry around, and simple to set up. For the sport flier, they're the way to go. Hi-starts are generally available in different sizes, for small or large planes. The Airtronics Launch Pail comes in a convenient plastic bucket. Davey Systems makes hi-start kits and sells the tubing and hardware separately as well. Craft-Air makes several sizes of hi-starts, including one specifically for small fields.

The other common method of launching is with an electric winch. The electric motor is connected to a drum with a coil of strong line on it. This drum acts as a flywheel, and can really exert a strong pull. The line runs out to a pulley staked into the ground at the downwind side of the field, about where you would stake out a hi-start. The line goes around the

Away it goes! A contestant at the AMA Nationals launches his Standard class sailplane. The winch tows it up to altitude and is released automatically. (Photo courtesy *Model Aviation* magazine)

pulley and comes back to the launch area. The pilot has a foot switch to turn the winch on and off. Sometimes another winch-like device called a *retriever* is attached to the line at the parachute. During the launch, the retriever pays out a light line; when the plane comes off the launcher, the retriever can reel the launch line back to the launch area.

Launching with a winch is similar to launching with a hi-start, but you have much more control over the process. With the plane firmly in your hand, tap the winch switch to build up tension. When you have it tight, release the plane and stand on the switch for the first part of the launch to build up speed. As you approach the top and the plane begins to nose over, release the switch and let the plane pull out more line. If the plane slows down, hit the switch and give it more pull. By pulsing the switch, experienced winch pilots can get much more altitude than can be obtained from a hi-start.

Winches can cost several hundred dollars, not counting the heavy duty 12-volt car battery it takes to run them. But most serious sailplane fliers feel

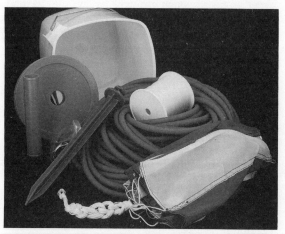

The Airtronics Launch Pail is a popular hi-start kit. The plastic bucket holds everything you need to get your sailplane in the air. Different models are available for lighter or heavier sailplanes. (Photo courtesy Airtronics, Inc)

that the advantages outweigh the problems. Clubs often have a winch that they set up for fun flying and contest practice. Davey Systems makes the most popular winch kits; there are several sizes available.

FLYING

When you take a new sailplane out to the field, the first thing to do with it is to see how well it will glide. Hold it over your head in your right hand, with the wings level and the nose pointing straight at the horizon. Take a few steps and give it a gentle push, straight away from you. Now fly it until it touches down. This will help you spot any tendency to turn, which could indicate a wing warp. It can also tell you if you need to add weight to the nose or tail of the plane.

Once you've launched, what do you do? Well, the first step is to trim your plane for hands-off level flight. Once the plane is flying itself with no help from you, start making gentle turns. You're looking for the disturbance that will be caused by flying through lift. Remember our discussion of thermal currents, and try to visualize a fountain of rising air. If there are buzzards or gulls in the area, they'll usually be soaring along in a thermal; they are a lot better at it than we are. I've flown in thermals with birds many times; they don't seem to mind.

If your wings wiggle, or the plane suddenly bounces to one side, that's indication of lift. Turn into it, and try to set up the plane in a tight circle. Don't get it so tight that the nose drops; most sailplanes are designed to prevent this. If you turn in the thermal, you'll go up. If the turn moves the plane to the outer edges of the thermal "fountain," where the air is falling, you'll come down. You'll be able to visualize this better after it has happened to you a few times.

You can't expect to get much thermal action your first few times up. Still, if you had a decent launch, it will take the plane three or four minutes to come back down. Think about where you want to land. Don't let yourself get in a situation where you have to dive at the ground, building up speed, in order to hit your safe landing area. Sailplanes will usually make good turns close to the ground, with

enough time to level the wings and land on the fuselage instead of a wingtip. Hand-tossing your plane will give you a good idea of how far it will glide in a landing.

THE ROBBE GEIER: AN UNUSUAL FLYING MACHINE

I've always had a fondness for the unusual in flying machines. That's a polite way of saying I dig weird airplanes. So when Robbe USA announced that they would be importing the Geier flying wing kit from Germany, I started making plans to get my claws on one. It's sold in two versions: a straight soaring machine, and with a pusher electric motor setup. Parts are included in either kit to mount a power pod and .09 gas engine on the wing.

I've built Robbe kits before, and have been very impressed with their thoroughness. Everything is clear and detailed. There are few places where things get lost in the translation. Speaking of which, don't be intimidated by the thick instruction booklet; it's printed in three languages.

The Geier is a flying wing with a pod out front. It uses elevons for control; the twin rudders are fixed. The pod makes it easier to balance the Geier by putting the battery pack and other heavy stuff out in front of the leading edge of the wing.

It's a fairly heavy airplane. You have to remember that the Geier E is a slope soaring machine, not a featherweight Old-Timer or thermal job. The electric power is there simply to give it a boost into the wind, *not* to let it float lazily on a calm evening. Nothing the Geier does is lazy!

Don't interpret that as a negative comment about the Geier. I have had a real blast with it, as soon as I figured out that it's designed to be thrown off an Alp. And it's great to have a plane that actually needs a windy day to fly! I'm an all-weather pilot now.

Construction

There's an extra plan sheet and extra pages in the instruction book that detail the modifications for the electric motor. Read these first; they affect the construction sequence.

Cindy Fetchko agreed to hold the Geier for a photo, but I couldn't persuade her to fly it! The electric motor mounts unobtrusively on a pylon at the back. Standard props are used; reversing the motor leads turns the prop in the correct direction. (Photo by Jennifer Pratt)

Two features that may take some getting used to are the metric measurements and the fact that the parts are numbered in the order that they're used during construction. A metric ruler is a must. If you take the time to sort out and identify the parts first thing, you'll find the numbering scheme an enormous help. Save all scrap pieces for gusset work later.

Be careful to get all the ribs 90 degrees to the building board. The wing is not fully symmetrical, so make certain you get the bottom side of all ribs down.

The instructions say to use contact cement for sheeting the wing leading edge; I trust Super Jet more. I had no problems getting the sheets positioned properly before the stuff went off. Before you begin sheeting, make sure the wing is flat against

the building board. This is your last opportunity to make sure the structure is warp-free. This is a good spot for sandbags. If you don't have handy weights, you can pin the structure down over the plans with pins through the spar webbing.

The wing joining instructions don't talk about dihedral, so I assume the wing is flat. I glued the light ply center rib to the right panel first with Super Jet, then trimmed and sanded it flush to the top sheeting. Then I used Super Jet to fit the other wing panel. Sand the heck out of the center section sheeting at this point. The fiberglass bandage that reinforces the center joint is pretty thick, so I used a sandable epoxy (Model Magic, to be specific) to attach it. I worked around the leading edge first, working the epoxy up through the fiberglass with a flexible-bladed palette knife, then across the top, around the tail, and up to the servo cutout.

Two evenings of work, and the hard part's done. The construction is conventional, so if you've ever built a wing of this type, it won't take long. The fact that all of the parts fit so well is a real timesaver—I never realized what a difference it made.

The instructions are a little sparse on the important point of aileron linkages. They tell you to bend the aileron torque rods, but they don't mention that you'd better have slipped the bearing tubes over them first! I cut one bearing tube in half and used a half for each torque rod. I drilled the ailerons to receive the bent end of the rod, trimmed the rod to fit the depth of the hole, and trimmed the leading edge of the aileron to clear the rod and support tube. There's a tiny gap there, but the ailerons move freely. Don't drill the hole for the rod too deep, since the aileron gets thinner the deeper you drill! I fitted the rods in place in the ailerons, attached the ailerons (I used D-Hinges, so the ailerons were removable), and then glued the bearing tubes in place. It isn't necessary to glue the torque rod into the hole in the aileron; it isn't going anywhere. You can no longer remove the ailerons at this point, so you might want to wait to do this until after you cover the wing. Finally, grab a fine sanding block and smooth this puppy out.

Now it's time to stick the fins in. This is when the Geier starts to look like something out of *Star Wars*. Don't forget to round the leading and trailing edges of the fins before gluing them in place. Mine were such a nice fit that I simply jammed them in and ran thin Jet into the joint—rock solid.

Elevon Mixing

The Geier comes with a sliding tray mixer. One servo moves the tray, and the other is linked to the elevons. The plastic tray slides on two metal rails. This is a perfectly good setup if your servos are the right size to fit the tray. Mine weren't. Ideally, I should have had a radio with a super transmitter that would allow V-tail mixing, such as the Ace Silver Seven or JR Century VII. I didn't. What I did have was an Ace Christy Mixer, a handy little box that connects between the receiver and the servos. I at-

tached it to the wing in front of the servos with double-sided tape, and just fitted the servos in solidly. You can't get any simpler than this setup, and you have full trim authority on both the elevator and aileron channels.

Electric Motor

The Robbe motor and prop included in the Geier E package are excellent. It's roughly an 05-size motor, as we reckon things in this country, but it really puts out the rpm on its eight-cell Sub-C pack. Incidentally, the battery pack is not part of the package, but it's very easy to solder one up.

I considered going to 800 mAh cells to save weight, and I may still try this. But I found that the Geier needed nose weight to balance properly, and rather than giving some lead a free ride, I went with the heavier batteries. The plans show the eight-cell pack with seven of the cells side by side and the eighth in a hump on top. To move the CG forward, I made two four-cell sets side by side, and attached them to each other with the four cells on top staggered back. With a little foam padding, it fits nicely far forward in the nose of the Geier's little fuselage. I stuck the flat pack for the receiver far forward under the drive pack, and still had room for the servo-mounted on-off switch and the receiver.

Flying

A charger capable of quick charging an eight-cell pack is necessary. Most of the fast chargers out are intended for six or seven-cell packs, so be certain your charger can handle it. My favorite chargers for electrics are the MRC RB-450 and Robbe's Automax 21. Both of these units automatically shut off when they detect peak charge, and the Automax is capable of fast charging 20 cells from a 12-volt source (see Chapter 1 for more details).

The first time I tried the Geier, I didn't throw it hard enough, skipped it off the ground, and snapped off the motor mount. No big deal; a little epoxy and we're back in business. This time, the strong right arm of a friend got the Geier a good start. Turns were solid, and control was excellent though lively. I got six minutes on that calm day, and realized that the machine had the flight characteristics of a slope-soarer.

So, next time, there was a 10-mph wind when I brought the Geier out. The little hot rod came alive, drilling its way into the wind from a running heave. This time I got eight minutes, and couldn't wait to go up and battle the wind again.

Several successful flights later, I decided to see how the Geier would do with more power. I latched onto a geared Astro Flight Cobalt 05. It fit the Geier beautifully. All I did was unbolt the gear drive, put it on one side of the Geier's motor mount bracket, and screw the engine to the other side using the same bolts. There's still plenty of gear mesh to run things. I used a Top Flite 11-7 prop for the first few flights. By the way, one pleasant surprise about this pusher setup is that you use standard props; you just reverse the motor power leads and bolt the prop on facing forward.

With the Astro cobalt 05, the Geier ramrods into the breeze with real enthusiasm. My motor runs are down to about five and a half minutes, but in that time I can really get some altitude. And with a good breeze, I'm getting flights in the ten-minute range.

The Geier is a lively little handful with superior penetration. You can turn it into the wind, put the nose down, nail it on a constant heading, and watch it gain altitude. Turns can be as tight as you please; I've never stalled it. If you have any experience with heavy slope soaring machines, you'll feel right at home. If not, fasten your seat belt and hang on! You'll enjoy the ride.

Chapter 5

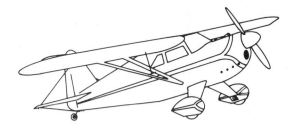

Scale Models

THE INTEREST IN SCALE MODELING IS TREMEN-
dous. It fits the reason that most people get into
the hobby. Most modelers appreciate "real" airplanes and they want their models to look like them.
They know that the planes they fly are just as "real"
as the big ones. Besides, you'll own a lot more
model airplanes than "real" ones, unless you're
Howard Hughes!

In this chapter we'll look at several popular
Scale kits of different degrees of difficulty. The in-
tent is to give you the benefit of some of the mistakes I made while building and flying them. The
techniques I describe will be useful in many different construction projects. We'll also talk about building from plans, if no kit of the plane you want to build
is available, as well as starting from scratch with no
plans.

NASA

One organization that you might like to get involved with in the course of your scale modeling ca-
reer is NASA, the National Association of Scale

Aeromodelers. NASA is devoted to Scale modeling
of all kinds: Control Line, Free Flight, and RC. They
publish a regular newsletter and maintain an excellent list of sources for scale data. You can get membership information by writing to NASA, c/o John
Guenther, RR 1 Box 715, Borden, IN 47106.

FAC

If little Scale airplanes appeal to you, let me introduce you to the Flying Aces Club. FAC is a
loosely organized group of ostensibly grown men
who share a passion for tiny models of old airplanes.
They tend to concentrate on Free Flight, but there
is a substantial amount of RC, too. Their newsletter is a gold mine of Scale data, tips, techniques,
and humor. You can get in on the fun by sending
$9 to FAC GHQ, 3301 Cindy Lane, Erie, PA 16506.
It's worth it for the "Glue Guru" column alone.

SELECTING A SUBJECT

There is a very large array of Scale and Scale-
like kits to choose from. You're certain to fall in love

with a few of them. But before you buy one and start on it, here are a few things you should consider.

How comfortable a pilot are you? If you're on your fourth or fifth airplane and you're confident of your ability, you can probably handle just about any Scale kit you can buy. On the other hand, if you've just crashed your first plane for the third time, you're a little more limited in your options for the next one. You should select a Scale subject with a strong consideration for how successful you're likely to be with it. If you're going to put six months of work into something you'll never have the courage to fly, I recommend plastic static modeling.

But don't be intimidated! There are planes that you can fall in love with that even a rank beginner can handle. They'll improve your building skills, deepen your appreciation for "real" airplanes, and then teach you new things about flying.

Here is a general rule: High-wing cabin-type air-planes are easier to fly than shoulder-wing or low-wing designs. As I said, that's a general rule, and it has many exceptions. But it's a real good place to start. So your first Scale subject should be a classic lightplane, such as a Piper Cub, Aeronca Champ, or Porterfield Collegiate.

SCALE KITS

Here is a partial list of some of the more popular scale model kits. There are more coming in all the time, so the best I can do is mention kits that have established a good reputation in my experience.

Top Flite Models produces an excellent series of warbird models. Many of these kits are designed by Hal Parenti, a world-class Scale modeler who has competed on an international level many times.

The Top Flite P-39 Airacobra can be built with optional retracts and flaps. It includes alternate color

This beautiful Dehavilland Comet was built by Keith Shaw. It's powered by two Astro Flight electric motors, and is capable of beautiful, graceful aerobatics. (Photo by author)

The Rearwin Speedster is a beautiful scale kit from Craft-Air. This charming plane flies as nicely as it looks on a .60 two-stroke or .90 four-stroke engine. (Photo courtesy Craft-Air)

schemes that are well-documented. The F8F-2 Bearcat can also be built with retracts; it requires a .60 engine. The P-40 Warhawk is one of the most popular .40 size Scale subjects, as is the P-47D Thunderbolt. The F4U Corsair comes with fuselage shells formed of balsa to speed construction; it requires a .60 and retracts. The P-51B Mustang comes with full-color decals; a conversion kit is available to change it to a bubble-canopy D version. The A6M2 Zero is one of Parenti's best; it builds into an outstanding plane requiring a .60 or a .90 engine.

Concept Models produces a Quarter Scale kit of the famous Fleet biplane that is an outstanding flier. The cabane struts are preformed, which saves a lot of trouble. It requires a large engine, such as a Quadra or Saito 270.

Craft-Air has come out with a kit of the Rearwin Speedster that is one of the most charming airplanes I've ever seen. There's enough Scale detail to please you, and the flying characteristics make it an excellent first Scale plane. It will fly well with a .45-.60 four-stroke. Craft-Air also makes a Scale model of the RV-4 homebuilt, a sleek-looking low-wing plane.

Flyline Models specializes in Schoolyard Scale—models that are small enough and fly slowly enough to operate happily in a schoolyard. We'll get

into these unique kits in detail later. Most are designed for .049 to .10 engines. The Flyline kits include the Kinner Sportster, the Fairchild 22, the Stearman C3B biplane, the Curtiss Robin, the *Spirit of St. Louis*, and the Great Lakes biplane. All can be built to "museum quality" detail.

Gee Bee Models makes a lovely kit of the famous British biplane, the Tiger Moth. All the cabane struts are prebent, which saves a lot of time. A .40 size four-stroke or .25-.30 two-stroke flies the Tiger Moth beautifully.

Great Planes Manufacturing makes several interesting scale kits. Their Cosmic Wind is just as fast and responsive as the full-size Formula 1 racer. Their AT-6 Texan is a .60-size plane that's easy to fly. The T-28 has a fiberglass fuselage and foam core wing; it's designed for .60 two-stroke engines. The Corbin Ace and Piper Tomahawk are Quarter Scale kits that fly very well, and would make good entries into Giant Scale airplanes. Finally, Great Planes has models of the famous Cap 20L aerobatic plane in several sizes. They fly just as snappily as the prototype.

Guillow is another company that specializes in small scale models. Their kits are very easy to build and fly very well. The Bellanca Cruisemaster is particularly impressive, with its triple fins; it's designed

The Fairchild 22 kit from Flyline Models is larger than many Schoolyard models; it takes an .09 to .15 size engine. The large wing gives it nice flying characteristics. It can be built with working shock absorbers in the landing gear struts. (Photo courtesy *Model Retailer* magazine)

for .049 engines. Guillow makes a Cessna 170 and Piper Tomahawk in the same size.

Jet Hangar Hobbies specializes in ducted-fan models. They produce kits of the Skyhawk, Mirage III, F9F-8 Cougar, and F-86F Sabre Jet. I've seen the Skyhawk and Mirage fly, and they are very impressive. The Skyhawk especially can be detailed beautifully with parts included in the kit.

Mark's Models makes a neat series of "Fun Scale" kits. These are snappy fliers that preserve the lines and markings of the prototype; they won't win scale contests, but they are fun! The line includes a Pitts Special, a Mustang for .40 engines, and a Mustang for .60s. Mark's also makes a line of precision scale kits, including a P-51D Mustang, an AT-6 Texan, a P-47 Thunderbolt, a Zero, and F4U-1A Corsair, an SBD-5 Dauntless, a Focke-Wulf FW190D, an F6F Hellcat, a Messerschmitt ME 109, and a PT-19 trainer.

Pica Products is well-known for their lovely Waco kits. The Waco is a big, handsome biplane. Pica has two sizes of Waco kits; one is designed for .60 engines, the other for .90-1.20 engines. Pica also makes a T-28B trainer with a nicely detailed canopy, an Aeronca Sedan that flies beautifully, a Cessna 182, a Focke-Wulf 190, a Spitfire, and a Bucker Jungmeister biplane.

Proctor makes two kits of the Nieuport biplane. These are craftsman's kits; among other things,

they feature spun metal cowlings. They also have two sizes of the popular Antic aerobatic Old-Timer. I've seen a lot of these at the flying field, and their slow flying characteristics have made them favorites.

Royal Products has a huge list of Scale model kits much too long to list here. They are all-balsa, and include very detailed plans with extra scale data. I've seen Royal kits built into fun-fly airplanes, and also turned out as detailed precision models. Royal kits include a Curtiss Hawk P6E, the Spitfire in two sizes, a C-47 Skytrain, a Ju 87D Stuka, a Staggerwing Beech, a Bleriot, a P-38 Lightning, a B-17 Flying Fortress that flies with four .20 engines, a B-25 Mitchell, and five sizes of Corsairs for engines from .049 to Quadra size.

SIG Manufacturing is famous for their scale models, and justly so. They have four different Piper Cub kits. Two feature the well-known J-3 Cub; one is for .40 engines, the other is Quarter Scale. The other two Cub kits are of the famous Clipped Wing Cub, the aerobatic plane made famous by Hazel Sig in airshows all over the country; it is also available in .40 size and Quarter Scale. Several of the SIG scale kits feature formed plastic fuselage sides that fit down over a crutch structure; these "Kwik-Bilt" kits are very durable and easy to detail. Kwik-Bilt subjects include a Cessna 150 and P-51 Mustang. The SIG Ryan STA is a precision scale model that has won national competitions. So has their Beechcraft Bonanza. The Smith Miniplane, Liberty Sport, and Skybolt are some of the most popular aerobatic biplanes around. Finally, their new Morrissey Bravo is a Quarter Scale model of a well-known American lightplane. It has become very popular for its smooth handling in the air and ease of transportation; both wings and the tail can be easily removed.

Simcoe produces several popular large scale kits of WWI planes, including the Sopwith Pup, the Fokker D-VIII, and the Fokker DR-1. They also have other designs that are available as partial kits. You get the plans and templates for cutting out the parts. You can supply your own wood or buy wood kits for each plane. Partial kit subjects from Simcoe include the Avia B534-IV biplane, the DeHavilland Leopard Moth, the Pitts S-1, the Cap 21, the Glasair homebuilt, the Scarab Jr. racing plane, the Zlin Z-50L, and the Nieuport 17.

Cressline has bought the scale kits that used to be produced by St. Croix Models. The subjects are unusual: the famous Burt Rutan-designed canard homebuilts, the Long-EZ and the Quickie. The kits are unusual too; they are amazingly complete. Every need has been anticipated, and the instructions take you through the entire construction process without neglecting the smallest step. The quality is absolutely amazing. I've seen the Long-EZ fly, and while it's not for beginners, it flies very well.

Sterling Models has been in business for a long time and produces several popular scale kits. Their Fokker D-VIII, PT-17, and Stinson Reliant are very popular; all are intended for .40 to .60 engines. Their Waco SRE biplane is also a popular kit; I've seen these with a lot of added detail, and they fly well with .60 engines.

Byron Originals is famous for their extensive

The Robbe SF-36 is a scale model of a Swiss airplane. It's a motor-glider; the motor is there to launch the plane, and is shut off in soaring flight. The Robbe model can be equipped with an on-board starter to duplicate this operation. (Photo courtesy Robbe USA)

The Cressline Long-EZ is a nearly scale model of a popular homebuilt aircraft. It flies beautifully on a .45 two-stroke engine and pusher prop; a retractable nosewheel is optional. This is a remarkably complete kit, with very detailed instructions. (Photo courtesy *Model Retailer* magazine)

line of scale models. Byron specializes: All of their kits are either giant models, or ducted fans, or both. The ducted fan line includes a C-2 Kfir, an F-16, an A-4 Skyhawk, an F-86D Sabre Jet, a MiG-15, an F-15 Eagle, and a BD-5J. They have no fewer than six different kits of Beechcraft planes: a Stagger-wing, three different Bonanzas, a T-34B, and a T-34C. Their giant scale planes include a P-51 Mustang with operating retracts and special prop, a P-47, a Zero, a Corsair, a Christen Eagle, a Pitts Special, a CAP 21, and the homebuilt Glasair. Byron kits are remarkably complete. If the kit requires special retracts, a special engine, or some other unusual accessory, Byron either includes it with the kit or sells it as an option. Byron kits are available factory-direct only. The cheapest of them is priced over $200, but they're well worth the cost.

Dave Platt Models is a small company that specializes in scale kits that can win competitions with no modification. Platt himself is a long time world-class competitor, and his kits reflect it. If you go to a Nationals or a Scale Masters event, it's odds-on that at least half of the kits in the top qualifiers will be Platt kits. The Platt line currently includes a Bucker Jungmeister, a Spitfire, a Messerschmitt ME-109, a Zero, a P-51, and a Focke-Wulf 190.

They will be releasing a precision scale kit of the Hawker Hurricane soon.

BUILDING SCALE KITS

Scale kits vary widely in the amount of prefabrication that you get. There are almost-ready-to-fly Scale models of planes like the Christen Eagle and Laser 200 which don't even need paint. On the other hand, "craftsman" kits such as the ones from Flyline Models come with part outlines printed on the wood sheets and blocks. Your first step is to cut out and shape your parts from this "printwood." Then there are semi-kits, like the line available from Wing Mfg., which include a set of plans and the foam wing cores.

A typical scale kit will come with die-cut or machine-cut wood parts, and perhaps a vacuum-formed plastic cowl, canopy, and wheel fairings. You should examine these parts if you can, or ask someone who has built one of the kits. Machine-cut wood parts are superior to die-cut, but will be more expensive because they take much longer to produce.

Stack-Sanding

Most die-cutting is of acceptable quality, but you

The P-51 Mustang kit from Byron Originals is remarkable. You can buy a complete power system for it, with engine, mount, and four-bladed prop. The landing gear and gear doors operate slowly, like the real thing. (Photo courtesy Byron Originals)

can always save yourself some trouble by punching out all of the ribs and stack-sanding them. This is done by stacking the ribs carefully, being sure that they are all right side up! If you're uncertain which side of the rib is up, look on the plans for a side view of the rib and lay the die-cut rib over the drawing. Once you have your ribs stacked, jog them together so that they're even and push straight pins through the stack to hold it in place. Push pins in near the leading and trailing edges of the ribs. If the stack is longer than the pins, push pins through from both sides.

Now load your sanding block with fine grit sandpaper, and lightly sand the stack along the top and bottom surfaces of the ribs. This will smooth out any rough spots on the surfaces that the covering will be attached to later. Be careful that you don't change the shape of the ribs in the process!

If the ribs you're working with are slotted for spars on the top and bottom, this is a good opportunity to make sure that all the spar slots are in the same spot. Push the spar stock into the slots in the rib stack. Use a sharp knife or sandpaper to adjust

the fit of the spar stock if necessary; it shouldn't require much. Be careful not to crush the wood when inserting the spar material.

Examine the leading and trailing edges of the stack. Check to make sure that the strip stock that will be glued to the ribs on these edges is a good fit. Some ribs have a V-notch cut in the leading edge, and the strip stock fits in the V cornerwise.

Now carefully remove the pins from the stack. Glance at each rib to see if any were cracked in the process, and use thin CyA glue to fix them if needed.

Molded Plastic Parts

It's a whole lot easier to fit a plastic cowl to the front of your fuselage than it is to carve out wooden blocks to the right shape. This is why most kits include a vacuum-molded plastic cowl. You'll often find that other shaped parts are molded from plastic, such as wheel pants, landing gear fairings, and canopies.

Most plastic parts found in modern airplane kits are formed from plastic that can be sanded. It's important not to use too heavy a grit of sandpaper, be-

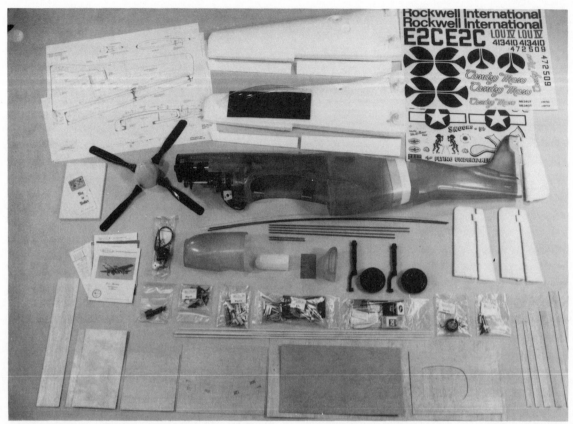

The deluxe Byron Mustang comes with engine installed in the fiberglass fuselage. The engine is geared to swing the special four-bladed prop. The wings and tail are foam, which can be covered with fiberglass and painted. (Photo courtesy Byron Originals)

Dave Platt Models makes several outstanding precision scale kits. They are competition-ready with no modifications. This is the Platt Focke-Wulf FW-190D. (Photo courtesy *Model Retailer* magazine)

cause you'll put deep scratches in the plastic that will be hard to remove. You should also be careful not to sand too fast, since the friction of sanding will build up heat that can melt or deform the plastic.

Vacuum-molded parts usually have to be cut free from the sheet they were molded from. Score the plastic lightly with a knife around the cut line and break the part free. Always cut wide of the part and sand it to its final shape, rather than trying to get an exact fit with your knife. Cut slowly, and use light pressure. Don't hold the knife in a death-grip; that can cause it to slip and go where you don't want it, especially around curves.

Once the cowl is cut out, hold it up against the front of the fuselage. I generally like to have the engine already mounted so I can cut the cowl to fit it. Remove material from the cowl to clear the engine, test-fitting each time you do.

When you have the cowl properly fitted, start rigging your attachment to hold it in place against the fuselage. Some kits do this differently, but most of the ones I've built use small screws. These fit through holes in the cowl into small blocks of hardwood glued to the front of the fuselage. When you attach these blocks, be sure to allow for the thickness of the cowl between the edge of the block and the edge of the fuselage.

Glue the cowl mounting blocks to the fuselage. Mount the cowl with masking tape, checking to make sure it's just where you want it. Then drill through the cowl into each block. Drill the holes as far from the edge of the plastic cowl as you can, so there's plenty of plastic between the hole and the edge. This will be the weakest part of the cowl attachment. I like to use the Ace Handrills for this step, since they're a lot easier to control than an electric drill. The bit size you use must be smaller than the diameter of the cowl attachment screw. When you have all the holes drilled, remove the cowl and enlarge the holes in the cowl with a larger drill. Don't just screw the screws through the cowl at this point, since you'll deform the plastic around the hole. The screws should fit easily through the holes in the plastic, and grip the wood beneath.

I put small washers under the screws before fitting them through the holes in the cowl into the attachment blocks. Don't screw them in too tightly, or you will weaken the plastic and crack it.

With the cowl in place, you can sand the joint between the cowl and fuselage to give you a perfect fit. Do this cautiously to avoid putting too much stress on the cowl. Model Magic Filler will build up the fuselage to meet the cowl if it's necessary. Model Magic also sticks to the plastic very well and can be used to fill deep scratches. If you're building up the fuselage side and don't want it to stick to the plastic, coat the part of the cowl that will touch the filler with Vaseline or light oil.

Finally, give the entire plastic cowl a light sanding. This roughens the surface slightly so paint will adhere better.

Edge-Gluing Plastic Parts

If your kit includes wheel pants or fairings, you'll often have to glue two fairing halves together along their edges. The secret to doing this is to sand the parts until the edges match evenly along their mating faces. You don't have to worry about leaving a ridge of plastic around the outside of the joint; this will come off easily after the halves are joined. But it's very important to get a good contact between the surfaces that are glued.

The method I use is simple. I tape a fresh sheet of fine sandpaper to a hard, flat surface like a tabletop or a small pane of glass. Then I cut out the parts and rub their mating edges on this sandpaper with a circular motion, a little at a time, testing the fit frequently. It doesn't take much to get a perfect fit.

You can use plastic cements, either liquid or tube-type, to fit these parts together, but I prefer to use CyA glues. Pacer Tech sells a glue just for plastics called Plasti-Zap that I've had very good luck with. A new product is PIC's Plasti-Stick, also a CyA glue designed for this kind of plastic. Both can be set off with accelerators and form a bond that is usually tougher than the surrounding plastic. Some kits recommend the use of methyl-ethyl-ketone, MEK, to bond plastic parts together. I don't use it because of the danger of getting some of the stuff in your eyes, which can cause blindness.

Once I have the edges glued together, I reinforce the inside of the glue joint with a strip of the plastic I trimmed off the part. You have to be careful with tight-fitting wheel pants, though, because this extra plastic strip could rub against the wheel when you mount the pant. Look at the plans. If you don't think you have enough room to use a strip of plastic, reinforce the joint on the inside with a bead of thick CyA glue such as Slow Jet. Hit the Slow Jet with accelerator to harden it.

Now you can sand off the ridge of plastic around the outside of the joint. Use a sanding block and fine sandpaper. Lightly sand the entire part to roughen it for painting.

Engine Mounting

If you plan to use the engine specified by the kit, then you won't have to pay any special attention to the way the engine's mounted; just do what they tell you. But if you have another engine in mind—say a four-stroke in a plane designed for a two-stroke—some changes may have to be made.

Lay out the fuselage plans and lay your engine on top of them in the proper position. This will give you a good idea of the changes you need to make. Perhaps the firewall is in the wrong place to hold the engine so the prop is in the right position. This can cause problems, and you might consider moving the firewall, depending on the shape of the fuselage; it's usually preferable to leave the firewall where it's shown on the plans and make some other compromise.

If the firewall is too far back, no problem. Just make a spacer of plywood sheet to the thickness you need and bolt it in place between the engine mount and the firewall. Longer bolts can be obtained at your

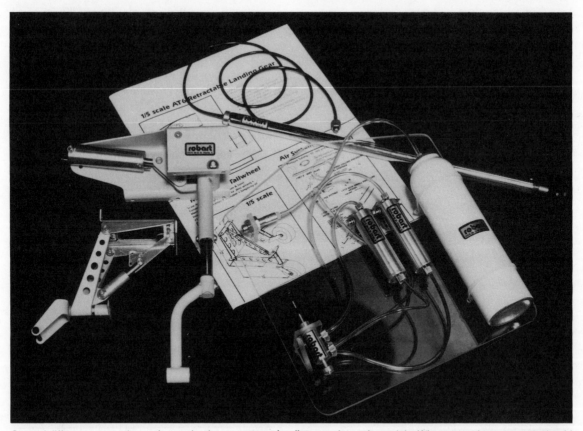

Several different companies make mechanisms to retract landing gear in scale models. When you select one, you should consider the size and weight of your model. This system from Robart is powered by compressed air; you pressurize the air tank before each flight. (Photo courtesy *Model Retailer* magazine)

hobby shop. Use blind nuts on the inside of the firewall, and glue the blind nuts in place so they don't pop off after the fuselage is all finished and painted.

If the engine is too long for the engine compartment, you might have to make some other changes. I've found that many of the scale kits I've converted to use four-stroke engines required no modification; the prop simply sticks out in front of the cowl maybe ¼ inch farther than the plans show. It's seldom noticeable, and certainly doesn't affect flight performance.

In extreme cases, if the engine you want sticks out an inch or more beyond the cowl, you may have to build a second firewall behind the first one. Make a copy of the firewall out of balsa sheet, and cut away the inside of it so that your engine will fit through with plenty of room to spare. Then make the second firewall out of ¼ inch plywood by tracing the cross-section of the fuselage at the point where the new firewall will fit. Cut it oversize so you can trial-fit and sand it to its final shape. Secure it inside the fuselage tightly, and fuelproof the entire engine compartment.

Mufflers

While we're talking about engines, this is a good time to plan the kind of muffler you're going to use. Figure this out now, before you have the cowl in place and cut to shape. Many four-stroke engines won't require the use of a muffler. However, if the engine is larger than a .45, you should have a muffler on it. This is especially true of the larger Enya four-strokes, which are very powerful and correspondingly noisier.

Several companies make lines of mufflers and adapters to allow you to fit the whole muffler inside a typical cowl, with just the exhaust protruding. You can often lead the exhaust out in the same place as the exhaust on the prototype. J'Tec has a muffler for every four-stroke made, mounted on adapters that allow them to be turned so that they exhaust up, down, or to the rear. Tatone Products also has an extensive line of in-cowl mufflers including one specifically designed for Pitts Special models. Check your local hobby store.

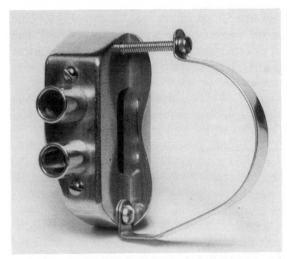

Attaching a muffler to an engine that's covered by a cowl on a scale model can be a problem. Several manufacturers, including J'Tec and Tatone, make in-cowl mufflers and manifolds to fit most popular engines. The inlet can be widened if necessary. (Photo courtesy *Model Retailer* magazine)

Planking Fuselage Sides

If you have a kit that requires you to sheet the entire fuselage, you will probably find it easier to plank it instead. Planking a fuselage consists of covering it with thin strips of balsa instead of bending a wide sheet around it. I've had good success with this method on curved fuselages.

I cut the balsa sheet into strips of ⅛ inch or slightly wider. Master Airscrew sells a balsa stripper that make this easy. If you don't have one, use a long metal straightedge and cut slowly so the straightedge doesn't slip.

I lay the first plank along the side of the fuselage. If there are stringers that are flush with the surface to be planked, I lay the first plank next to one of them. More often, the stringers are meant to be covered with the wood sheeting, so I start by gluing the first plank over the stringer running down the middle of the fuselage side. Then I work from either side of this first plank, fitting new strips in place against the old ones. I sand the new strips at a slight angle along the edge that will make contact with the last plank so there will be a better surface fit. You have to fit the plank along its entire length, and taper it toward the tail. Touch a drop of glue to the formers beneath the plank, then run a line of glue along the edge of the plank and fit it in place.

When you near the top, you'll be cutting smaller and smaller pieces to fill in the remaining empty space. Don't try to bridge gaps with glue; if a part is too small, cut another one. Use plenty of glue, and wipe off the excess as it oozes out.

Most people will tell you not to use CyA glues for planking, because they harden harder than the wood and leave ridges when you sand. So aliphatic resin glues such as SIG-Bond or Titebond are preferable. But if you don't have the patience to wait for them to dry (I don't), you can solve the ridge problem easily. After the planking is all in place and the glue set, sand the fuselage with wet-or-dry sandpaper that has been moistened with Z-7 Debonder or Jet De-Solv. It'll take the ridges right off and leave you with a smooth surface.

Whatever glue you use, you'll have to sand the finished fuselage to get rid of the edges of the planks and round them out. It'll go quickly, so use a light grade of sandpaper. Once you're through, you'll have a very strong, rigid fuselage.

SCRATCHBUILDING

Suppose you've always wanted to build and fly a particular airplane, but there aren't any kits of that plane available—or the kits you've seen aren't of the make and model you want to build. What then?

Well, there have been literally thousands of plans published over the years. Many model magazines publish two or three plans each month. Modelers save back issues of their magazines for just this reason. Since most magazines print their plans on an as-ordered basis, you can count on all the plans they've ever published still being available. If you can get an issue with the construction article in it as well as the plans, you are two-thirds of the way to having a kit!

Call or write to any of the model magazines listed in Appendix B at the back of this book. They'll send you complete lists of their plans and prices for them. They will also give you an idea of whether or not they have the back issues you need.

Once you have the plans you want, start figuring out how much wood you'll need. Make a list of the sheets and sticks called for. Now visit your hobby shop and pick up the wood.

The most time-consuming part of building from plans is cutting out the pieces. You'll need to use some method to transfer the shape of the piece to the wood. For a part that will be duplicated quite a bit, such as the wing ribs, I make a template out of stiff cardboard, like a file folder. Tracing around the template gives me my wing ribs.

There are several ways to transfer the pattern of other pieces, such as fuselage formers, to the wood. Some people push pins through the plans into the wood to mark the outline of the part. Others buy two sets of plans, cut out each part, and paste the paper to the wood. I like to use a sheet of carbon paper to trace the part outlines onto the sheet wood. Whatever method you use, cut the pieces oversize and sand them to final shape, checking them over the plans.

Pay careful attention to the grain direction of the wood as you lay out the pieces. The grain should run from the front to the back of each wing rib, and from the top to the bottom of each fuselage former.

Cut and shape all your parts before you start construction. You won't want to stop in the middle of construction to cut out more parts. Once you get 'em together, it'll be just like building a kit.

Building without Plans

Of course, it's possible to build Scale models without any plans at all. You don't have to be a draftsman to do it, either. You do have to do some research, but that's part of the pleasure of a Scale project.

Is scratchbuilding cheaper than buying a kit? *Never*. There's a lot of waste in scratchbuilding. Furthermore, when you buy the wood in quantities of two or three sheets, you pay a lot more than the same wood bought in a kit.

Beware; you might get bitten by the contest bug. Will you be disappointed if the plane is not competitive? Prepare yourself emotionally for using the first plane as practice for a *really* competitive one.

I talked to Bob Underwood about building Scale. Bob has been on several international RC Scale teams, and placed second in the world a few years ago with his fabulous Hiperbipe. He's working now as Technical Director of the AMA, and is acknowledged as an expert on Scale modeling. Here are some of his pointers:

Research

Collect all the references and documentation on your plane that you can. Bob says, "I've seen a lot of people build something that proves that their documentation is wrong." You can't collect too much material on your subject; it seems like when you're halfway through, you always discover more material about the airplane. Don't glue a stick until you're comfortable with the amount of material you have. This means that you should have all your questions answered about all the exterior dimensions of the plane.

Sources for Documentation. Bob has several favorite places to look for documentation. "I haunt newsstands and look through full-scale magazines. Most large bookstores have big thick volumes on historical aircraft of all sorts. Even though I might have no immediate interest in the plane, I save the book or article . . . I guess I'm a frustrated librarian."

You don't really find much in general public libraries. College libraries, especially if the college has an aeronautical department, are good hunting grounds. Look out for foreign publications, too.

A company that specializes in aircraft books of all kinds is Zenith Aviation Books. They publish a regular catalog full of valuable reference books and information. Write to them at the address listed in Appendix B.

Bob haunts the local airports—not the major ones; he seeks out the little private fields. You'll be surprised at what you find in those shabby little hangers; you might come across a privately owned example of the plane you want to build. If you do, a camera will get you the best documentation in the world.

Ask around at airports to see if there's one of "your" airplanes in the area. Most owners are delighted to talk to you about the plane because they have the same kind of interest and pride you will have when your model is done.

The Experimental Aircraft Association in Oshkosh, Wisconsin, has an extensive library. The EAA emphasizes homebuilts, warbirds, and antiques, all of which make excellent Scale model subjects. Their museum is worth the trip to northern Wisconsin. If you can make the trip during their annual Fly-In, you'll see more operating historical and homebuilt aircraft at once than anywhere else in the world.

Historical Aviation Album is a small business that publishes excellent reference material. Their address is in Appendix B. A letter will bring their list.

Don't ignore full-scale aeronautical publications. TAB Books has hundreds of titles on aircraft of all kinds, including the excellent Aero and Detail in Scale series. Their catalog will give you valuable sources.

How about the aircraft companies themselves? You can write to them; addressing your letter to their Public Relations Department is probably the best bet. Many will never respond. Smaller companies will respond much more often. Treat them like precious gems; return their letters with thanks. Homebuilt aircraft companies will often be able to sell you a package of plans and pictures. This will certainly give you everything you need to build an accurate model, so it's worth the price.

Coordinating Your Information. Once you've accumulated your data, spend as much time as you can studying the details of the plane. If you have more than one three-view drawing of the plane, they'll probably differ. Look for those differences, and search both text and photos to try to find clues on which is correct.

Color. While you're at it, decide on the color scheme you like the best. This decision should be influenced by the quality of your information, and on the kind of finish you plan to use. If you plan to paint, you aren't limited to the colors available in iron-on coverings. On the other hand, painting is more difficult than using an iron-on, so if you can pick a set of colors that's available in iron-on coverings, you might want to go with it. If your plane was covered with cloth, think seriously about using an iron-on fabric such as Permagloss Coverite.

Color is probably the hardest thing to get precisely right. If the aircraft is from before WWII, you won't find any color photos. Even if you do, they generally are not accurate. Even today, a slide or negative will produce different colors depending on where and when it was printed.

Plastic modeling publications are excellent sources for color data. Plastic modelers are trying to solve the same problems we are, and they work just as hard at it.

Be certain to find a description of the colors; you just can't tell from color photographs. Remember that early photographs are all on Verichrome film, which doesn't register reds well. When Bob built his Lockheed Alcor, he had pictures showing that it was painted black with white markings. One photo showed a man standing in front of the plane wearing a white shirt. When you look at the picture, it's obvious that the markings weren't white. Bob eventually found a man who worked at Lockheed, and he discovered that the trim color was yellow.

If you can locate old color charts, hang onto them. Find out what brand of paint was used on the prototype. Go to your local paint store. DuPont has a color chart that cross-reference their colors with Piper and Cessna.

Plans

If you aren't a draftsman, don't attempt to draw a set of plans. You can use other techniques to produce something to build from.

For example, you can project a 35mm slide and draw it on big pieces of paper. If you have a drawing of the plane, you can use an opaque projector. Bob uses this method. He tapes paper up on the wall, projects the drawing, and backs the projector off across the room until he gets the size he wants. Keep it true by making sure the projector is pointed straight at the wall. Bob checks this by drawing a right angle in the corner of the plan he's projecting. If the angle is 90 degrees on the projection, it's true.

Don't mix drawings when you project the plane. Pick the one that's the most accurate and stick with it. You don't want to build one version of the front half of the plane, and another of the back half. Picking parts of different drawings is a sure way to get yourself hopelessly fouled up.

How Big?

You're going to have to decide how big to make the plane at this point. The decision will be governed by different considerations, such as the engine you want to use, and the size of the vehicle you'll use to transport it. The size of spinners and wheels you can buy is important . . . you don't want to have to scratchbuild your own spinner. The style of the wheel is important. A vintage plane might have spoked wheels or wheels with very thin rims. Williams Brothers makes classic style wheels in several sizes. Fulton Hungerford makes beautiful spoked wheels that are sold by Peck-Polymers. You can find these in hobby shops, or check the addresses in Appendix A for these companies.

Make your plane as big as you can and still be practical. Bigger planes fly better and will carry more detail. Bob says, "My first Wittman Bonzo was built at a scale of 2 ½ inches to the foot, and it flew like a lead sled. Someone saw it and commented, 'If you make it bigger, you could make it lighter.' At first, I thought he was crazy. Then I realized he was talking about wing loading. I built another Bonzo to a scale of 3 inches to the foot, and picked up a lot of wing area, with proportionally less weight. The new plane is much bigger than the old, weighs a pound and a half more, and flies great."

Hiding the Engine

Some airplanes don't lend themselves to concealing model engines. You have to put the engine somewhere, and you'll probably have to put a muffler on it, too. The bigger the plane, the easier it is to put in the engine.

If you're building a vintage plane with an exposed engine, the size of the cylinders is important. You can buy fake cylinders in several different sizes from Williams. Plan your model so that you can use these. If it's impractical, try making a fake cylinder or two from balsa dowels. If you like the way they look, make enough to build your dummy engine.

Lay your outline on a table and put the engine on it. Now do the same with the spinner(s) and wheels. Now is the time to make any changes to the size of the plane.

Cowling In Engines

You need to plan for the way air is going to flow over your engine when it's hidden inside the cowl. Design it to direct air over the cylinder of the engine. Figure a large space for the cooling air to exit. There should be several times more exit opening than entrance. The engine heats the air, so the volume of air exiting is greater than the volume of air entering. You can direct the airflow with pieces of aluminum sheet. Don't just put the engine in a great big hole. The air will enter and pool inside the cowl. This can lead to an overheated engine very quickly.

Material Selection

The natural inclination is to make scratchbuilt planes a lot stronger than they have to be. The average person almost always overbuilds.

Remember, the lighter you can make it, the better it will fly. A box made out of ⅟₁₆ balsa sheet will be nearly as strong as one made from ⅛ sheet, and much lighter. Use hardwood and ply as little as possible. Firewalls, bearers for the landing gear, wing spars, and wing joiners are about the only places you'll need something stronger than balsa.

Building

Bring your kit building experience into play. Steal and borrow from kits for construction techniques. Bob borrows airfoils from kits that have flown well.

Enlarge the stabilizer to improve the flying? It's seldom necessary. Bob says that if it looks right, it'll fly. His record backs this up.

Plan your interior structure. Does the fuselage show stringer outlines? It's easier to build a box with stringers on the outside than stringers and formers. Foam wings can show rib outlines with cap strips. Draw them in on the layout. Plan your spars. Figure out control runs. This is where your kit building experience comes into play.

According to Bob, "25 percent of your time is figuring out how you're going to do it; 50 percent is doing it. The rest is undoing what you did wrong because you didn't spend enough time planning the first 25 percent."

Crutch Fuselages

Bob has developed an excellent way to build straight fuselages. He goes to a hardware store and gets a piece of aluminum tubing, ¾ or 1 inch in diameter, nice and straight. Then he makes a reference line down the center of the fuselage on the plans. He figures all the bulkheads from this line, setting them up so he can drill a hole down the center of each. When the bulkheads are cut out, he drills the hole to fit them over the aluminum tube. After drawing vertical and horizontal reference lines on each bulkhead, he slides them onto the tube, holding them in place with tape. He lines up the reference lines, cuts light ³⁄₁₆ balsa-strips, and starts planking at the reference lines. One plank goes on each side of each line, sighting down them. He sands the edges of the planks to fit squarely. When the fuselage is almost done, he removes the tape, closes up the sides, and removes the tubing. It's impossible to build it crooked. Once it's built, you can sand a lot off the ³⁄₁₆ planks.

This method is good for turtledecks of almost any shape. Mount the tube in a vise to hold the fuselage in any attitude. The structure can't warp in spite of variations in the wood; by the time the tubing comes out, it's a rigid piece. If the tail tapers too far to get the tube through, build it back as far as you can and build a tail piece.

THE GOLDBERG PIPER CUB

The Anniversary Edition Piper Cub from Carl Goldberg Models isn't a precise Scale model, but who cares? It was intended to be a plane that a beginner can fall in love with and succeed on. It does that job with style and class.

Your first impression of the Cub kit is that it comes in one heavy box! There's a lot of wood in there. Fortunately, a good part of it is scrap from the die-cut sheets. The cutting is excellent, and it will take very little smoothing of the edges to get clean parts. The kit contains an absolutely complete hardware package. All that's missing is an engine, radio, tank, and wheels.

I decided to do my Cub a bit differently. Any popular .40-size engine will fly the Cub beautifully. For an old-fashioned plane with a lot of wing, a four-

The Piper Cub kit from Carl Goldberg Models is a classic. It's engineered with the first-time builder in mind; though it's complex, the instructions are excellent. The flying characteristics are as nice and gentle as the full-size Cub. (Photo courtesy Carl Goldberg Models)

stroke is perfect. The Saito .45 is the ideal engine for the Cub. I decided to use two of them. Well, not quite, but that's what it looks like. I installed a Saito .90 Twin, a working twin-cylinder four-stroke that consists of two .45 cylinders over a common crankcase. It is way too much power for the Cub, but those two cylinders look perfect. As it turned out, the Saito .90 runs so smoothly at low speeds that it was just right for the Cub—but I never fly at more than half throttle!

I had to make one major change to accommodate the big twin engine. The Saito .90 comes with a radial engine mount on the back that is intended to bolt to the firewall. It's not possible to move the firewall in the Cub forward, since it interlocks with the fuselage sides, so I needed a spacer. The center of former D makes the ideal spacer size. The punched-out sections from the fuselage sides and the larger formers make up the rest of the spacer. Glue eight of them together in a stack, and shape the sides of the stack to the shape to the center of former D. The stack should be an inch high to put the prop where it belongs out the front of the cowl.

Cut a slot in the top of the spacer to clear the carburetor fuel line. Test-fit the engine on the spacer to make sure you have it right. Attach the spacer with Super Jet or other thick CyA glue, and drill the hole for the fuel line as soon as the spacer is glued in place. The spacer should touch the top of the fuselage.

A DuBro fuel fitting makes life a lot easier. This fitting is a small brass item that goes in the fuel line between the tank and carb. You can plug your fuel pump into the fitting, which allows you to fill the tank by shutting off the outlet to the carb. I installed one in the lower right side of the fuselage.

Trimming the cowl is surprisingly easy. Work from the back. I cut away more than was really needed on the rear, just to find out where it needed

The Saito .90, with the wood spacer bolted to it, attaches directly to the Cub firewall. It needs to be right up at the top of the engine compartment, so drill the holes for the fuel line and throttle pushrod before installing it. (Photo by Jennifer Pratt)

to be cut away in the front of the cylinders. If I had it to do over, I'd leave more material back there, but this way looks okay, especially when the engine compartment is painted black. A slot has to be cut in the top of the cowl to clear the two needle valves; remove the needles while you're fitting the cowl.

Onboard Glow Plug Battery

I decided to install a system to heat the glow plugs from an onboard battery when the throttle was at idle. This will always allow you to idle the engine reliably at lower rpm, since the plugs won't get blown out by the fuel mixture. As it turned out, the system wasn't necessary to get a really good idle, but it makes it much easier to start the engine!

I decided on the Nilite 3 system from Ace RC to power the plugs. The Nilite has some very nice features. You turn it on and off with an external switch. There's an external charging jack for the battery. This jack does double duty; not only can you use it for charging, but you can connect an external battery to the glow plugs directly through this jack.

The Nilite 3 system uses Head Lock glow plug connectors, just like the ones on the famous McDaniel Ni-Starter, but smaller. You push them onto the plug and turn them ¼ turn. They stay until you turn them back.

The switch that turns the plug heat on and off is in a little box that's open on one side. A rod feeds through this box from one side to the other; this connects to the throttle servo output arm. Inside the box, a tapered brass plunger sits on this rod and is held in place with a set screw. When the throttle servo goes to idle, this plunger moves over the switch and turns it on.

I mounted the Nilite switch behind the throttle servo on the side of the fuselage. The switch box is on a standoff so I didn't have to bend the pushrod. The throttle doesn't require much throw at all, so it can be hooked to an inner hole on the servo output arm.

Wing

The die-cutting on this kit is so precise that building the wing is really just a matter of assembling it. When you sand out the trailing edge of the wing structure, before attaching the triangle stock that forms the trailing edge center section and wing-

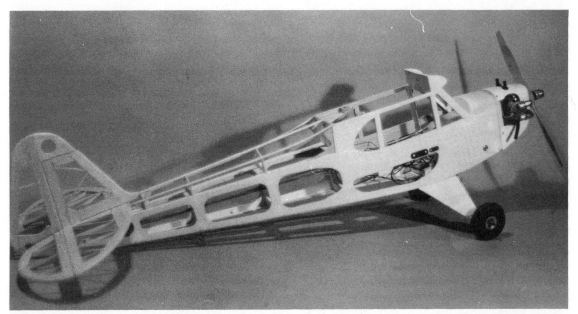

The tail structure glues onto a platform at the rear of the fuselage. It's easy to get it straight. The turtledeck over the rear of the fuselage is made of small dowels glued into slots in the formers. The servos attach to rails that fit into slots in the fuselage walls. (Photo by Jennifer Pratt)

tips, make certain you haven't sanded an angle into the edge. It's easy to do, even with a sanding block. If this edge isn't straight, the wingtips and center piece will be at an angle rather than continuing the proper shape of the wing, and it will be very difficult to align the ailerons properly. If it's extreme, it could affect control by acting like a wing warp.

Pushrods

I used flexible Sullivan pushrods instead of making up the pushrods shown on the plans. This necessitated adding three braces to keep the tubes from flexing. It was very easily done with leftover balsa sheet. I installed a sheet at the rear of the radio compartment and drilled two holes to line up with the servo arms. Then I inserted the pushrod tubes through these holes.

Engine

It's important to set up the throttle linkage so as to get full travel. You won't need full throttle, so if you can't get all the throw, concentrate on the idle end.

I had run the Saito .90 Twin on the bench for at least an hour, just to familiarize myself with the engine. I discovered that it's really not hard to set the two needle valves. You can't do it by ear, of course; in fact, sometimes it's hard to tell that both cylinders are running! Feeling the exhaust will tell you if you have a dead cylinder; hot means it's running.

Anyway, I had it turning up to 8000 rpm on a Dynathrust 14-6 prop, and idling at 2000 rpm without plug heat. When I first ran it after installing it in the Cub, I couldn't get that good an idle without losing one cylinder. I'd richen up the cylinder that was dying, and the other one would quit. I chased that weak cylinder from one side of the engine to the other, and finally settled for an idle of around 2500 rpm for my first flight.

Then, on the advice of a friend, I tried examining the glow plugs. I removed both of them, and plugged them each into a Ni-Starter. When I held them side by side, sure enough, one was dimmer than the other. I bought half a dozen plugs and tried

them all until I found two that looked alike when they were glowing. Once I stuck them in the cylinders, my weak cylinder problem disappeared.

Flying the Cub

The first flight was prefaced by the above-mentioned tinkering session. When I was satisfied with the engine, I pulled it out of the restraint and started taxiing. I didn't have a low enough idle to satisfy me, but thanks to my grass field, I didn't have a problem with the plane taxiing away. Ground handling was fine. One tends to hold full up elevator while taxiing to give the tailwheel every chance; oddly, I found that it made tighter turns with half up instead of full up.

The entire first flight was conducted without advancing the throttle stick more than halfway. At two clicks above idle on the stick, low passes were a symphony. The Cub flew beautifully, handling the crosswind with only a tad of rudder.

After a couple of those gratifying passes, my ears detected that the weak left cylinder had conked out. Advancing the throttle slowly to half, I made a complete approach on the right cylinder. Since I had a gusty crosswind, I idled the engine, fed in left aileron and right rudder, and found myself slipping the little baby in authentic Cub style. Still on the right cylinder, I landed, turned, and put-putted the length of the runway. Sigh.

On the second flight I ran out of fuel at an embarrassing spot. I had richened the left cylinder, and at least they were both running right up until the end (with no plug heat). I made a turn after the engine quit and looked pretty good for a deadstick landing until a scrubby tree reached up and grabbed the Cub. The left wing mount block was torn out and the rear window plastic cracked. On the other hand, the tree lost that branch. It took a lot less time to fix the Cub than it will take that tree to regrow that branch!

I decided I wanted more elevator throw on the basis of that deadstick landing. There was no indication that the Cub was falling off on a tip in the turns, and I believe I could have stretched the glide out of the reach of that tree if I had had a tad more up. So I moved the elevator snap-link up to the second hole from the top.

Since discovering the trick of matching glow plugs, flights with the Cub have been sheer joy. It's so solid, I've begun using it to test new radio systems. The engine has run through two gallons of Red Max 10 percent four-stroke fuel, and is now starting on a gallon of Cool Power. And I'm still taking off at one-third throttle.

SCHOOLYARD SCALE

The term "Schoolyard Scale" is supposed to have come from the fact that these little slow-flying planes can be flown in an open space about the size of a schoolyard. In fact, school athletic fields are perfect spots for them—nice, smooth grass to land on, and only an occasional goalpost or soccer net to avoid. There aren't any other distinquishing characteristics of the class, no defining measurements like the 13-inch maximum wingspan that defines Peanut Scale. Schoolyard ships are defined by being small, cute, and easy to fly. What could be better?

I've built three or four Schoolyard jobs. They aren't all that difficult to find; there have been some excellent plans published for them in many different magazines. Don Srull has designed a handful of excellent Schoolyard planes that have been published in *Flying Models* and *Model Aviation*; any of them would be suitable for your first venture into this class. Slightly harder to find, but well worth the effort, are designs by the Grand Master of model airplanes, Bill Winter. You can come up with some real classics of Bill's in *Model Airplane News* issues from the 1950s and '60s. If it was originally intended for a Galloping Ghost or Ace RC pulse-rudder radio system, it'll make a fabulous Schoolyard ship with a modern lightweight RC set and micro servos.

Flyline Models produces a whole series of Schoolyard-size kits. Most of their planes are designed by Colonel Hurst Bowers, a master builder of small models who now serves as Curator of the AMA Museum. Flyline kits seem pricey, but the sort of wood you find in that box doesn't come cheap; it's among the best wood I've ever seen in a kit box.

Power for Schoolyard Planes

Flyline kits are designed for .020 or .049 glow engines. The current crop of Cox engines will suit them perfectly. Using a Cox .049 for a Flyline kit like the Megowcoupe will give you a sweet-flying machine, and you can buy Cox fuel and parts everywhere.

Because I love out-of-the-ordinary (read *strange*) modeling stuff, I have used different power for my last two Flyline kits. I like Diesels. For some reason, they haven't caught on in this country, but they're a big deal in Europe. Diesels are available over here, but you have to look for them.

It's worth the trouble. A Davis Dieselized Cox .049 will swing an eight-inch prop as happily as can be, and run longer on a tank of fuel than the glow version. Davis conversion heads are available for an enormous number of different engines, and Davis fuel is among the best.

I've been running several small Diesels from Europe. The P.A.W. Diesels are made in England and imported by two American outfits: Eric Clutton, 913 Cedar Lane, Tullahoma, TN 37388; and Carlson Engine Imports, 814 East Marconi, Phoenix, AZ 85022. A buck sent to either of these gentlemen will bring catalogs and info sheets. The P.A.W. 80 is the same size as an .049, but it has the neatest little carburetor you've ever seen. It throttles beautifully! A P.A.W. in a Flyline kit, with a third channel on the throttle, is a true gem of an airplane.

I acquired a couple of very special Diesels at a Toledo Show a few years ago. This chap was sitting at a table in the Swap Shop area with the tiniest little engines. I glanced, then did a double take; the heads were square! These little gems are made by a Czechoslovakian gentleman named Pfeffer, and the heads are machined out of bar stock. The Pfeffer Specials are around .036 displacement, and turn a 7-4 prop happily. To top it all off, you can buy a Pfeffer Special with a carb. It was love at first sight, so I acquired a couple from the seller, who turned out to be noted engine collector Arne Hende. Arne had come to the Toledo show from his home in Sweden.

With two Pfeffer .036 engines in my hot little hands, I had the perfect powerplant for the .020-size Flyline kits. I've flown the Flyline Inland Sport with a Pfeffer, and it was a dream . . . takeoffs from grass,

This Stinson Voyager is a Schoolyard Scale kit for .049 engines, made by Micro-X. It is very lightweight and flies slowly—just the thing for small fields. (Photo courtesy *Model Retailer* magazine)

touch-and-goes, slow flying, with the Pfeffer sputtering away for almost 20 minutes on a ½ ounce tank. In this day of Giant Scale, the little yellow Inland popped a few eyeballs.

Pfeffers are relatively rare, and likely to stay that way, since Mr. Pfeffer is getting on in years Carlson has a few for sale. So does Stu Richmond, who writes about engines for *Model Builder* magazine. I never miss his "Engines of the World" column; he wrote about the Pfeffers late in 1986.

Building Techniques for Schoolyard

Schoolyard models are very similar to Free Flight ships in that they're inherently stable and quite lightweight. In fact, my Inland showed its FF heritage one day when I launched it without turning the receiver on. (It did great for about two minutes, before a tree grabbed it.)

Building a Flyline kit means working with printwood. You'll be cutting out the parts yourself. With fresh blades in the knife, this is no big deal. Cut outside the lines and sand down to them. I like to cut out all the parts of whatever assembly (wing, fuselage, tail) I'm working on, then assemble it.

Fuselages are open structure. The great trick with these is to build the sides on top of each other with a sheet of waxed paper in between. When you're building the second side over the first, try

to place your pins where glue won't get through the hole made by the pin and reach the lower fuselage side. That's a good policy anyway, since thin CyA glues can firmly glue the pins into your building board if you get sloppy! Remove the pins with a turning motion to free them.

Don't yield to the temptation to jam in the crosspieces without first sanding the ends to a good fit. Even with gap-filling CyA, a structure where the ends of the crosspieces don't fit well into the corners and joints will be much weaker than one where some care is taken on this. If the plans show a crosspiece going directly into the angle of a joint, sand the end of it to a point, and keep reshaping the point until it fits. That's the main reason to cut the pieces at least 1/16 inch too long!

Save all scrap sheet to make gussets. These little triangular pieces are very important to the overall strength of the framework. Be sure you put them in where they're shown on the plans. If the plans call for them, the designer had a good reason for it, you can bet.

I have several tools that make building with light wood much easier. The sharpest knife you can get is important, and the best one I've ever found is the Uber Sciver. *Model Builder* magazine sells these knives. They have a surgical blade, sharpened to a compound edge and held in place with a drawbar chuck. This means that the blade doesn't come loose when you cut around a curve. For delicate work there's nothing better. I borrowed a trick from model railroaders and bought a thick black rubber block for a cutting surface. This keeps the wood from slipping and doesn't hurt the blade when you cut through. Finally, you're going to do a lot of sanding. A sanding block is essential. I could make up a set of blocks with different grits, but I'm lazy. The Wedge Lock sanding block uses a sanding belt; you slip it over the block and lock it in with a sliding wedge at one end. Since you can get sanding belts in really fine grits, the Wedge Lock is just right for this kind of work.

Sand out the printing on the wood if it's going to be on the outside of the fuselage; it will show through the covering.

Joining the sides is a crucial step. Do it over the plans. Make shallow cuts in the fuselage sides where the plans show ''crack line'' and carefully crack the sides, so you can pull the sides together at the front. Now cut the crosspieces to exactly the length shown on the plan. Glue the hardwood gear mount crosspieces in place, watching to see that you're lining them up straight. Then pin the fuselage down on the plan top view, using these pieces to hold it in place. Now carefully add the other crosspieces, checking the trueness of the fuselage at each step.

Covering and Finishing

The key to a sweet-flying Schoolyard job is lightness. You should put on the lightest finish you can. This means tissue and dope—or it should. But once again, I'm far too lazy for that. I use Micafilm.

It seems like for every modeler I find who swears by Micafilm, I find two that swear *at* it. I had a frustrating time with it too at first. Then I dis-

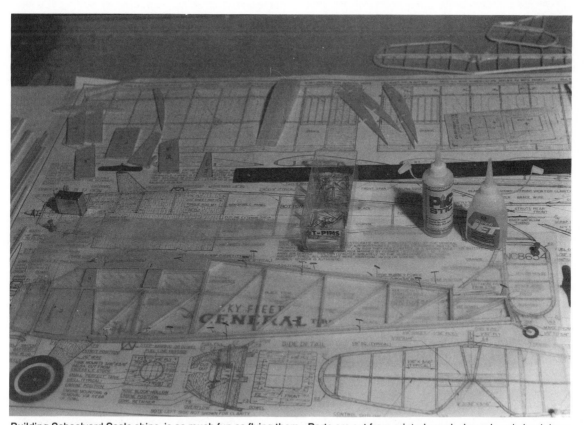

Building Schoolyard Scale ships is as much fun as flying them. Parts are cut from printed wood, shaped, and glued down over the plans. Square balsa cut to length makes up the structure. When one side is built, you lay a piece of wax paper over it, they build the other side. This ensures that the sides are identical. (Photo by Jennifer Pratt)

covered the secret of Micafilm: Read the directions! I had my iron set way too hot.

Micafilm doesn't have adhesive on it; that's one of the reasons why it's so light. You paint the structure with Balsarite wherever you want to stick the Micafilm down. Micafilm shrinks. If you have your iron set at a temperature that causes it to shrink, it's very likely to shrink away from the surface of the structure before the adhesive cools down enough to grab. Set your iron at 220 to 250 degrees, and the Micafilm will go on like butter on toast.

THE COVERITE CHESTER JEEP

In the late 1920s and early '30s, air racing was where the action was, and brilliant and eccentric people were showing the world some weird and wonderful machines. I can't think of a better way to appreciate the era of the great racing planes than by building a model of one of them. One of the pleasures of the sport of aeromodeling is this sensation of touching history, of making it yours.

Coverite has produced a series of semi-scale kits from this era, including the Gee Bee Model D and Model E. These are classic kits that build into great-flying models; I've built 'em and flown 'em for years. The most recent kit in the line is the Jeep, the

Art Chester's unusual little racing machine.

The kit itself is all you could wish, considerably superior to the previous Coverite kits. It's not for rank beginners, since the instructions are a bit muddy in spots. The wood is excellent, and the hardware package is complete. Coverite has vastly improved the die-cutting; parts are cut very cleanly. Each part has its number clearly marked on it—a real time- and frustration-saver. Good die-cutting is important, since the wing shape will depend on where the holes are cut in the ribs. I didn't even have to sand any of the rib edges—that's precise.

You'll appreciate the parts organization in the kit. Sheet and stripwood are taped together in bundles, and there's a cloth "goodie bag" of small stuff that's much more convenient than the usual stapled plastic bags.

The wings are unusual, to put it politely. They have a strange shape no matter which way you look at them. They're straight on top, and at the bottom they widen from the fuselage to the point where the struts attach. Then they taper from the struts to the tips. To achieve this, you have to shape the spars so that the die-cut ribs sit at the correct angles.

Begin with the rear spars. You mark the locations of the two end ribs and rib #9, which is the wide point of the wing. Then you mark ⅜ inch down

The Jeep, a famous racing plane built and flown by Art Chester in the 1930s, is the latest scale kit from Coverite. Even though it's an average-size model, it's over Quarter Scale! The model flies fast with a .40; it can be flown with a .20. (Photo courtesy Coverite)

from the top at the outer ribs, so the spar will be ⅜ inch thick at those points. A diagonal line is drawn from the ends of the spar to the center, and the wood under the line is trimmed and sanded away (a belt or disc sander helps). This gives you two spars shaped like very shallow Vs. Finally, you taper the inboard ends of the spars to make it easier to join the wing panels together. Be absolutely certain before you do this that you have the spars positioned correctly, so that they will join with the flat side to the top.

You can save yourself quite bit of trouble by stacking the ribs and drilling the holes for the aileron pushrods before assembling the wing. If by some chance you didn't think of this in time (like me), you can make yourself a handy little hole punch by sharpening the end of a piece of ¼ inch brass tubing. Use a knife to remove material from inside one end until it's sharp. Notching it in a couple of places can help saw through dense parts.

When you have the spars shaped, the ribs are slid on the rear spars. It's a good idea to sand the spars slightly to make this easier. Push the ribs onto the spars by holding your fingers against the rib on the front and back of the spar and pushing gently. Don't get upset if they break; just lay them flat on a piece of waxed paper and glue them back together. When all the ribs are on the front and back spars, sight along them to make sure that the panel is as straight as you can make it. Twisting gently at this point before the ribs are glued can help prevent wing warps later. If you have a warp that you just can't get out, twist the wing so that the aileron edge is twisted up so you have built-in washout.

I recommend planking the leading edge of the wing rather than sheeting it. It's a lot easier to fit nice, thin planks into that in-and-out leading edge than trying to shape a sheet of wood to it. (More on planking later.)

Fuselage Construction

I used a thick cyanoacrylate glue (Slo-Zap, Slow Jet) on the former halves. Work slowly and make sure that you have the correct ones; this can be confusing. Another view on the plans would have been helpful. Cross-piece location is unimportant as long

as they touch the sides and don't interfere with other parts later.

I'm a four-stroke freak, and a plane like this should have one. Any .40 to .45 four-stroke would be dandy; from personal experience I can recommend the Enya .46 (for a lot of power), the Saito .45 (a beautiful-running engine), and the O.S. .40. I installed the O.S. Because I had to adjust the firewall position to accommodate the engine, I didn't fit the firewall when told to by the instructions. I glued F-1 and F-3 in place, then glued the tail ends together and added the other formers.

I found what must have been a slight goof on the plans. They show the ply fuselage doublers glued flush against F-3, where the only place they could fit is against F-2.

Take the time to make sure you have the right parts before you glue. This is especially important for the tail feathers, which are somewhat unusually shaped. The forward piece of the vertical fin is a small one. Look for the edge that matches the curvature of the leading edge of the fin.

I've struggled with sanding blocks for a long time. I've tried gluing sandpaper to blocks (pain in the tush) and tried to get regular sanding blocks to hold a strip tightly. It ain't hopeless, but it's close. No more, thanks to the Wedge Lock, the sanding block that wears a belt. You just buy belt sander belts at your neighborhood hardware store. They're available in all different grits. They slip onto the Wedge Lock and fasten tightly in seconds. You can change them instantly. The rounded front makes it easy to work around curved parts. Get one. Why make things harder than they have to be?

Fitting the stab is much easier if you draw a centerline down it. Measure the leading and trailing edges and mark the line from the front to the back. Using this line, eyeball it into position. Then measure the trailing edge to make sure that the distance from the end of the fuselage to each stab tip is the same.

Planking

Planking the fuselage is masochistic fun. Cut a piece of the 1/16 sheet to the width of the bay you're planking. Then cut strips off this piece, one at a time.

I used a Master Airscrew Balsa Stripper to make nice, uniform planks. Fit each piece in place between formers and braces. Use Jet or similar thin CyA glue to secure the planks. Thicker CyA, such as Super Jet and Zap-A-Gap, fills in the holes. It goes quickly, and with a reasonable amount of care and a touch of sandpaper afterwards, you'll have a smooth Scale surface.

You should be cautious not to sand the planked surface too deeply, since the glue doesn't sand as well as the balsa. If you wind up with a ridge of glue, try wet-sanding with a fine piece of wet-or-dry paper and Z-7 Debonder. This can feather out the ridge in short order.

Continue the planking out to the rudder hinge line. It's easier if you shape the planks to wedges, tapering out to the hinge line, before sticking them down. They don't have to be perfect; your faithful Wedge Lock will smooth them out to perfection after they're all in place.

Once all the planks are in and sanded, fill in the dings with Model Magic Filler. No, Model Magic isn't just spackling paste like you get in hardware stores. It sticks better, and it's much stronger. Most important, it won't pop out of a hole when the wood around it flexes. It's worth what it costs.

Two tips for working with Model Magic Filler: First, get yourself a flexible-bladed palette knife. (They're sold at art supply stores, but ask your hobby dealer first.) They're the greatest for working the filler into the tiniest cracks. The palette knife is also the world's best method for applying epoxy.

Second, stir the Model Magic Filler. In fact, you should beat it like meringue. Just work up the bit you're going to use. If it seems dry, add a drop or two (no more!) of water. Try these tricks, and filling the planking on the Jeep will be like frosting a birthday cake (you can tell I'm hungry, can't you?).

Once the filler dries, pop a finer grit belt on your Wedge Lock and smooth it out. It feathers out beautifully with a gentle touch.

Hinge and attach the tail surfaces at this point. I used Goldberg hinge slotting tools to dig out the slots for solid nylon hinges. The elevators are fitted first, and the first thing to do with them is measure them for joining. The wire joiner has a horn on it, and you'll have to cut away the edges of the elevators to give you space for the wire and the horn. Drill 3/32 holes into the elevators for the joiner wire ends. Be careful not to drill out the sides of the elevators. Ace RC's hand drill set makes this job (and a lot of others) a snap.

Glue the hinges into the rudder and elevators, but not into the fin and stab, so the tail surfaces are removable. This will come in handy later to make covering easier.

Install the pushrods now before sheeting the bottom of the fuselage. I recommend Sullivan rods. Route them out the rear of the fuselage now; the open bottom will let you make a neater job of it. Support them halfway back. When it comes time to install the servos, you can make a support with holes cut in it to hold the outer rods in place in the servo bay. There's all kinds of room in there.

The rudder control horn should be mounted a little lower than shown on the plans so that it clears the elevator when the elevator goes down.

If you plan to fly inverted at all, it's a good idea to allow for as much down elevator travel as possible. There's plenty of space for it, but if you anticipate it now, you'll come out with a neater installation.

I used CyA glues throughout. Not that I have any prejudice against epoxy, but I've gotten spoiled by the super glue accelerators. On that subject, I find that Goldberg's Jet Set works a little slower than Pacer's Zip Kicker. This allows you a bit more time to make sure that everything is aligned properly before things kick off, without sacrificing any gap-filling capacity. I keep both on hand and use them where their differences do me the most good.

I left the firewall installation until last (before planking over the top forward section of the fuselage) because I needed more room for the O.S. .40. The engine installation must be precise, because it has to stick out of the opening in the plastic cowl just right or the spinner is going to rub against the cowl. As a result, the technique I used is a little involved. If this intimidates you, stick with the K&B .40 shown on the plans and follow the relevant instructions exactly. I find that the four-stroke is worth the trouble.

To begin with, all fuselage formers except the firewall should be in place. This makes certain that the fuselage holds its proper shape. The first former also provides you with an accurate measurement of the shape of the plastic cowl.

With the engine attached to the engine mount, I fitted the firewall slightly behind the marks I made earlier on the inside fuselage sides, and held the engine mount against it. Then I slipped the cowl over the front. Next, I found the best position for the engine mount on the firewall. You have to make sure that the firewall bottom is flush against the fuselage bottom sides while doing this. Mark the position of the engine mount on the firewall and remove the whole business. Now tack-glue the engine mount to the firewall. Next, put the whole business back together and look for the best position of the firewall in the fuselage. You can't get much down or right thrust on the engine because of the cowl; it has to fit closely to the backplate of the spinner. Check at the position of the prop driver to see that the spinner will fit properly. It isn't as hard as it seems. Just keep remembering the beautiful sound that four-stroke will make when it putts by you.

Once you've marked the firewall position, remove everything and drill the firewall for engine mounting bolts, fuel lines, and the throttle pushrod. I used 6-32 hardware and blind nuts for the engine mount. Be sure to put lock washers under the bolt heads when you install the engine mount to prevent loosening from vibration. Put the firewall back in position, with the engine mounted on it, and check its alignment again. Now Super Jet the firewall in place. Remove the engine mount, epoxy the firewall in on both sides, and fuelproof the engine compartment with a coat of Balsarite.

The first few engine runs showed that I needed better cooling, which is logical because of the size of the four-stroke as opposed to a standard engine. I created more exit area for the airflow by cutting away the bottom of the firewall and the bottom fuselage about an inch back toward the tail with a Dremel tool. I removed about ¾ inch of the firewall, then I filled in the opening in the tank compartment with sheet balsa and fuelproofed it. Problem solved.

I installed two gizmos to make life easier: a DuBro Kwik-Fil fueling valve and a McDaniel Ni-Starter Adapter. The Kwik-Fil was fitted through a ¾ inch hole drilled in the lower left side of the engine compartment where it would be unobtrusive. The Ni-Starter Adapter projects through the cooling vent right behind the cowl, so that I have a safe place to reach to remove the glow plug batter once the engine is running.

Install the battery and fuel tank, and pad them thoroughly. Install the throttle pushrod. Install the ¼ × ⅛ top stringer. Now plank the top of the fuselage over the tank. It's still accessible through former F3.

Plastic Cowl

This part may appear tricky, especially since the instructions just gloss over it. Actually, it's easy to shape the front of the fuselage to fit the cowl outlines.

Start by sanding the flange off the rear of the cowl. Now glue two strips of ¼ inch square balsa to either side of former #1 on the front of the fuselage. Position them so that they are set back from the edges of the former by the thickness of the cowl. The cowl should fit over these pieces and be almost flush with the fuselage sides; you'll have to taper the sides to their final shape (matching the cowl) with your trusty Wedge Lock. Now glue a piece of ¼ square to the bottom of Former #1, and shape a piece for the top of the former to hold the cowl in place from all four sides.

Now you can decide how you want to attach the cowl. For an attachment that doesn't show from the outside, you can install a hook on the firewall, epoxy another hook on the inside of the cowl, and run a rubber band between them. I chose the easy way out and put two small screws on either side through the cowl and into the ¼ square balsa. Don't overtighten these screws or you run the risk of cracking the plastic. Washers on the outside are a good idea.

Fitting the Wing

You will probably have to sand the wing saddle a bit to fit the wing exactly. A little care now pays off big later. The wing mounting blocks also need to be shaped a little to fit snugly against the leading edge of the wing. I fitted the two plywood tabs for the wing mounting bolts as shown on the plans, then sanded them even with the leading edge.

Two Ace RC tools greatly simplified this task, the Handrills and the Tap Set. You don't have to be a serious builder to own these; they're so inexpensive that there's no excuse *not* to get them. Each set is worth about an hour and a half of your time and frustration.

I aligned the wing exactly by measuring from the tips to the tailpost, then drilled a hole through the left ply tab into the wing block. I then enlarged the hole in the wing and tapped the hole in the block. With the wing held firmly in place by the left bolt, I drilled and tapped the holes for the right. Presto— one wing, mounted.

Mounting the Clear Plastic Canopy

Mounting the canopy can be tricky, but it's worth the trouble to get it right. Start with H5 snug against F5 and resting against the top wing sheeting. Fit each H1 to the curve of the wing, and then against the fuselage side forwarded of the leading edge. Take your time here; this shows later. Flubs can easily be corrected with Model Magic Filler.

Fit H3A and H4 in place, using the two plywood canopy bow pieces to measure the exact location for H4. Then fit the top longeron into the notches with H3 flush against F3, and start planking.

Wheel Pants

I wasn't nuts about one feature of the wheel pants. The wheel pant halves in the Gee Bee kits released earlier by Coverite nest together; you glue them together and sand off the ridge. The Jeep pant halves have to mate perfectly. You glue them together after making sure you have a perfect match. This seems like an unnecessary pain to me, and also doesn't provide as much gluing surface as I'm comfortable with.

I sanded the halves to mate as near to perfect as I could before getting impatient. Then I glued them together with Plasti-Zap, which works great

and is very strong. Finally, using strips of plastic that had been cut off the edges of the cowl and pants, I reinforced the inside of the glue joints at the front and rear. Make certain when you do this that you have adequate clearance for the wheels later; they're a tight fit. Finally, I used Model Magic Filler to smooth out the glue joint on the outside. Moisten the plastic a bit to improve the adhesion of the Model Magic.

I didn't have a flanged Fox wheel collar as specified in the instructions, so I proceeded as follows: After fitting the balsa landing gear fairings and drilling the hole on the inside of the pant, I slid the pant on the axle, followed by a wide wheel collar. I then inserted the wheel and slipped it on the axle. Finally, I fitted another wheel collar over the axle up inside the pant by sticking the collar's set screw on its wrench and using the wrench to maneuver the collar. It's close quarters. It makes it a lot easier if you use an oversize wheel collar here. If the inner collar is of the right width, it centers the wheel in the pant. The whole shebang is held in place with the outer collar.

Now glue the pant to the outer axle and balsa fairing with Model Magic Epoxy. The Model Magic can be sanded smooth easily after it sets up, and is very easy to work into shape. Check the alignment of the pant before the epoxy sets up. Make sure it's perpendicular with the fuselage when viewed from the front and side.

If you look at photos and drawings of the Jeep, you'll see a teardrop-shaped fairing on each wheel pant that fairs the landing gear into the pant. This is very easy to duplicate with Model Magic Filler and a roll of fine sandpaper. Harden the Model Magic fillet with regular Jet. The filler is porous, so this process works very well.

Covering

The Jeep was covered with cloth, so I used Cream Permagloss Coverite and painted the cowl, spinner, and wheel pants with Black Baron Epoxy, which matches the Permagloss. Another avenue you might take is covering with Super Coverite (white), adding a coat of primer, then sanding and painting. The Black Baron spray paint is recommended; I've also had good results with SIG Skybrite and this method.

Cover the horizontal stab first, leaving a lip of covering extending over the stab-fuselage joint. Then cover the rudder and glue its hinges in place. Cover the bottom of the fuselage. Now each side of the fuselage can be covered with a single sheet of Coverite by cutting a slot in the Coverite for the stab and draping it over the side. Start applying heat at the center and work outward. Don't rub the iron; put it down and lift it. I covered the landing gear struts with Permagloss just to save paint.

The canopy is also covered with a single piece of cream Permagloss, slotted to clear the windshield bow. The seam behind the bow will be covered with black paint, and hardly shows anyway. It's a lot easier task than it may seem thanks to the high shrink of the Coverite. I painted the windshield bows and the cockpit area black. The area beneath the forward windshield is painted black to prevent glare from blinding the pilot.

Detailing is a piece of cake. The only improvements I could suggest would be thinner window material and decals for the green stripes on the fuselage sides.

Trace the window patterns onto the clear plastic with your knife (an Uber Skiver, of course). The window panels will break easily along the score lines. Each piece will have to be trimmed for a perfect fit.

Wilhold RC-56 glue is the classic for gluing windshields, since it dries clear. But if you're careful, you can use Super Jet. Other super glues and accelerators I've tried on window material have fogged the plastic, so be sure to test whatever you're using on scrap first. I fitted the forward right panel first. I trimmed it until it fit smoothly along the fuselage joint and rested against the forward bow. Then I tacked the corners down with Super Jet, one at a time, checking alignment carefully. I sprayed a shot of wife repellant . . . I mean *Jet Set* . . . on one surface and applied the glue to the other to get a quick set. Once the corners were down, I applied fillets of Super Jet followed with Zip Kicker, being careful not to let the Super Jet run out of the joint. Then I trimmed the plastic to the edge of the rear

windshield bow, and along the forward bow. The left windshield piece was attached the same way, with the edge glued to the forward bow trimmed to just touch the right plastic panel.

The rear windshield piece was fitted over the back edges of the two forward pieces. I aligned it as carefully as I could, then spot-glued it in the center front and back. Then I glued the corners and filleted. Finally, I trimmed the plastic off flush with the back of the rear former.

I finished the whole thing off with yellow ¼ inch Goldberg striping tape covering all joints and outlining the entire windshield. I used a small brush and Black Baron Cream to paint the tape to match everything else. A drafting pen made nifty fake screw heads. And it wasn't nearly as hard as I'd though it would be; the whole process took about two hours.

I made the green fuselage stripes with a sheet of Trim Monokote, the self-adhesive kind, although regular Monokote would work fine. I cut two strips of it large enough to cover the stripes shown on the plans; then I sandwiched them face-to-face under the plans and pinned the whole shebang to my building board. With my faithful Uber Skiver (you need a *really* sharp knife for this trick) I cut through the sandwich, following the plans, from the front to the back. I put Scotch tape down over the plans as I want to save 'em for possible later use. Hey, presto— green stripes!

Thanks to Coverite's Brushable Black Baron paint, which matches the Permagloss, the wheel pant detail is a piece of cake. I used Tamiya Acrylic for the green, and fuelproofed it with a coat of Black Baron Clear. You can cut masking tape for the arrow down the middle of the green stripe, or freehand it like I did and correct your flubs with a brushful of the other color. Remove the gear to make it easier to steady your hands.

Be sure to protect the decals with a shot of Black Baron Clear, especially on the wings, where the covering flexes.

Wing Struts

The struts are straightforward. I made one modification: Instead of screwing the strut bases to the fuselage, I stuck a pin through the strut into a hole in the fuselage. You can count on the two screws in the wing ends of the struts to hold them in place. This way, if the wings flex, as in a hard landing, the ends of the struts don't tear out. I finished the struts with thinned Model Magic and brushable epoxy.

There are a couple of different ways to approach the canopy hold-down. The kit recommends making a hole in the wing sheeting, installing a hook, screwing another one to a ply plate on the inside of the canopy, and using a rubber band to keep the thing in place. I fitted Goldberg nylon brackets to the inside front of the canopy and the back. They snap over screws. The canopy fits pretty tight, so it doesn't need a lot to keep it aligned.

Flying the Jeep

I set up the O.S. .40 with 10 percent Red Max fuel and a 10-6 Master Airscrew prop. (I generally use Master Airscrews because they're fairly heavy and many four-strokes idle better with them because of the flywheel effect.) I tuned the needle with the cowl off, leaving it rich. Incidentally, I had clipped the knob off the needle and soldered an extension to it which extends through a hole in the fuselage side.

The only surprise encountered in flying the Jeep is the fact that it likes to carry what looks like a lot of up trim. I suppose this is because of the long nose moment and fairly heavy engine. There are no ill effects, and the little ship has no bad habits. I've done everything with it but spin, and it handles beautifully in all regimes. I suppose it would spin if I moved the CG backward, but why fool around with such a little beauty?

The O.S. .40 four-stroke has plenty of power, even slobbering rich. After flying the Jeep for a while, I wasn't surprised to learn that Henry's prototype is still flying with a Veco .19. Certainly any popular .40 or .45 four-stroke will be beautiful in the Jeep. Whatever you pick, you'll be glad you took the extra time to install the engine with the sound that fits the plane. This airplane is the stuff of dreams. Take it out and polish the pylons with it.

Chapter 6

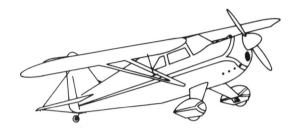

Giant Scale

THERE HAS BEEN TREMENDOUS INTEREST IN giant model airplanes over the last few years, and it's increasing. The reason is obvious: These big beasts are impressive! While they may take no more real work than a finely detailed smaller model, a big model just naturally looks like more effort went into it.

Giant model airplanes have some special requirements that the builder has to be aware of. They require stronger materials, bigger engines, and more care in construction than many smaller models. If you're a beginner, don't start out with a giant model. You need to accumulate building and flying skills before you try one of these. You'll put too much money and effort into a giant model to risk it in the hands of an inexperienced pilot, especially if that pilot is yourself!

If you're ready for the "giant step" into big models, however, you will find that most giant models are easier to fly than their smaller counterparts. They move more slowly, giving you more time to anticipate the plane rather than simply reacting to it. They have bigger wings, and if they are built properly (meaning "without excess weight"), they have very satisfying flying characteristics.

AMA LIMITS

The AMA Safety Code states that the maximum allowable weight of a model airplane is 55 pounds. This doesn't mean that there aren't people flying heavier models. It does mean that such models are flown without the benefit of AMA insurance. Because of this, most flying fields don't allow over-55 pound models to fly.

I don't know of any giant model kits that weigh over 55 pounds, so it's unlikely that most sport fliers will ever build one. Frankly, the largest model I can imagine wanting to build wouldn't weigh that much. There's controversy over this weight limit, and I don't know how it will be resolved; I do know that there are a lot of excellent giant models that weigh well under the AMA limit.

RADIOS FOR GIANT MODELS

Selecting a radio system for a giant model requires some special attention. You should get the most reliable system you can find. This means that you should plan to spend over $200 on the system; you can't buy the kind of reliability you want for less. Forget the "sport" or "house brand" radios for giant model work.

You can use standard-sized servos for the throttle and for switches like the retract controls or ignition kill switch, but the flight controls must have heavy-duty servos. You will probably need a servo for each aileron, one for the elevator, and one for the rudder.

A receiver battery of at least 1200 mAh capacity is essential. These servos are going to be working a lot harder than the ones in your sport models. This means that they'll use up the battery pack faster; the power has to come from somewhere! One approach to solving this problem is to use a separate battery pack to power the receiver. There are several devices to make this possible. The JoMar Glitch Buster has this option, as well as solving the problem of interference received in the servo cables themselves. If you put a servo on each aileron, you will have to run long wires through the wings to each servo, and these wires make pretty good antennas. The Glitch Buster isolates all servos from the receiver with optical coupling. Using a standard 500

Giant models need special hardware to stand up to the extra stresses and strains imposed by their size, weight, and power. This steerable tailwheel assembly uses a leaf spring and two attachment bolts; it's made by C.B. Associates, which has a large assortment of stuff for giant models. (Photo courtesy *Model Retailer* magazine)

mAh pack to power the receiver, then connecting a Glitch Buster to the servos and powering them with a 1200 mAh battery is as close as you can come to a bulletproof setup. I've used it with excellent results.

ENGINES FOR GIANT MODELS

When giant models first came along, modelers were forced to convert chainsaw, weed-cutter, and other small gasoline engines to power their models. This usually involved milling off excess castings to reduce the weight and overbalancing the flywheel to cut down on engine vibration. Such modifications take skill and special equipment.

Now, however, there are several fine engines available specifically for large model use. Some are "conventional" glow engines, such as the Super Tigre 2000 or the Saito 270 twin four-stroke. I lean toward using these engines and others like them in giant models, because you can use all that you've learned in handling glow engines in smaller models. The Saito 270, for example, will develop as much power as a popular gasoline-powered engine like the Quadra. There's also the fact that you will have to get special equipment and learn new techniques for handling gasoline, which is much more dangerous than glow fuel. On the other hand, gasoline is much cheaper than glow fuel—and available at a lot more places!

If you use a gasoline engine like a Quadra, Sachs-Dolmar, Kioritz, or Kawasaki, your safety procedures need to be different. Gasoline isn't as friendly as alcohol. Prohibit smoking anywhere near your plane or supplies. Use only an approved-type gas can to transport the stuff. Be certain that the tank and fuselage are vented; vapors can build up to an explosive level in a fuselage. Keep a fire extinguisher handy. These are safety practices that full-scale fliers use; we need them for the same reasons.

Your plane should have a servo-operated kill switch on the engine. Since magneto-driven engines can start easily, this safety switch is a sensible precaution.

When you start the engine, have a helper holding the plane. Switch the ignition off. Choke the engine according to the engine instructions; close the

This Kioritz is typical of the gasoline engines used in some Giant models. It incorporates an engine mount and a magneto. The special in-cowl muffler is made by Tatone. (Photo courtesy *Model Retailer* magazine)

choke valve and pull the prop through. It should take eight to ten flips. Now set your throttle to a few clicks above idle, switch ignition on, and start flipping. When the engine pops, open the choke halfway. Once you get things running, open the choke all the way after the engine has had a chance to warm up.

I often see people flipping props on gas engines with their hand, with or without a heavy glove. Frankly, this scares me. I always use a chicken stick; J'Tec makes a heavy aluminum stick with a shaped handle just for giant engines. I can get just as powerful and fast a flip with the stick as I could with my hand, and if the engine backfires, I don't get hurt.

Don't adjust the needle valves on a gas engine until it's had a chance to warm up to operating temperature. Adjusting the needles on a gas engine is similar to procedure used on glow engines (see Chapter 7 of *The Beginner's Guide to Radio Control Sport Flying*, TAB Book No. 3020). I generally start with the idle rather than the high end. Once that's established, I slowly open the throttle and lean out the high end until I get maximum speed. Then I back the needle out at least ½ turn, so that the engine is running rich. Don't let the engine run for

long periods on the ground at full speed; you could overheat it.

GIANT MODEL KITS

Many companies are manufacturing giant model kits. SIG Manufacturing makes one of the all-time favorites, the Quarter Scale Piper Cub. You can't do any better than the Cub for your first giant model; its sweet flying characteristics are legendary. Furthermore, you can power it with a conventional two-stroke .60 engine, although a four-stroke 1.20 would be more satisfying! O.S. makes a beautiful twin-cylinder four-stroke engine, the Gemini, that is perfect for the Cub.

Other companies that make giant kits include Great Planes, Bridi, Ace RC, Jim Messer, Circus Hobbies, and Byron Originals. Great Planes makes a splendid Piper Tomahawk kit with a fiberglass fuselage. Jim Messer makes several beautiful scale kits. Ace RC's giant kit is the 4-120, a 1.20-sized version of their popular four-stroke sport planes.

Byron Originals' giant kits are worth some special attention. They have an extensive line of giant models. Byron has a policy of offering everything you need to complete one of their models except the radio. This means that they have done a lot of research on engines, power systems, mufflers, retract systems, engine mounts, and a hundred other details. I've found that they know what they're talking about, and the easiest way to guarantee success is to buy their customized accessories.

The Byron Glasair is a 30 percent reproduction of a popular homebuilt aircraft. It gets a lot of attention for its snappy looks and outstanding aerobatic performance. This would be an excellent first giant kit.

The Glasair fuselage is hand-laid fiberglass, as are the wheel pants. The wings and tail surfaces are polystyrene foam. Everything is indexed to the other parts, so misalignment is unlikely. The wing panels come with the wing spars in place. This builds into a plug-in wing system that makes the Glasair very easily transportable.

It's very easy to get into the Glasair. The top hatch hinges out of the way, and the firewall removes from the front with a few bolts. A universal engine

The Glasair is a Quarter Scale model of a popular homebuilt airplane. The kit, from Byron Originals, is an excellent choice for your first giant model. The wing sections are removable, and the entire engine mount and firewall can be removed for easy servicing. (Photo courtesy Byron Originals)

mount accepts Quadra, Tartan Twin, Super Tigre S-3000, Saito 270, or similar large engines.

The latest addition to the Byron line is the Seawind, a scale model of an amphibian airplane. It carries its engine on a pylon attached to the vertical fin, well away from the water. The Seawind is a smooth, sculptured-looking plane.

One remarkable thing about the Seawind is the optional retract system. It consists of watertight retractable wheel mechanics, a retractable water rudder, and sequencing gear doors. If you install this setup, you'll not only be able to take off and land from a runway, you could land on the water, flip the gear down, and taxi up on the beach! This is a remarkable achievement in itself, and even more so when it's mass-produced in kit form.

THE CAMBRIA SKYVAN

One unique giant scale project that I've enjoyed very much is my Shorts Skyvan. The Skyvan is a charmingly homely airplane in use around the world

as a transport capable of using unprepared landing fields. The one I built is kitted by Cambria Models, a British company that is just beginning to be distributed in the U.S. It's an outstanding kit.

The scale of the Skyvan kit allows it to be flown with relatively small engines. Two standard .40s will fly it well. I selected two Enya .46 four-strokes, since I'm very familiar with them. They produce an honest ¾ horsepower each, so I was sure they'd fly the Skyvan as well or better than a pair of two-strokes.

I added a couple of things to the Skyvan kit—a steerable nosewheel and a lighting system. The lighting system gave me navigation lights, landing lights, and wingtip strobes, all switchable from the transmitter.

Construction

The Skyvan is the most complex model I've attempted in all my years of butchering balsa, so I admit I was a bit intimidated. I mounted all three plan

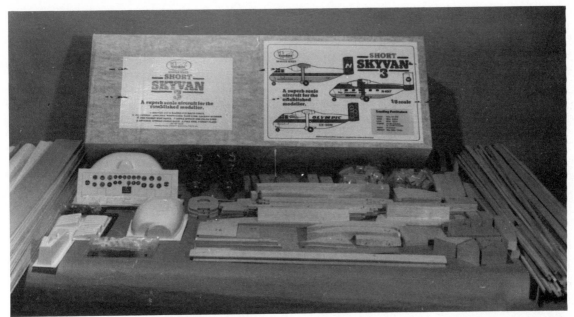

The Skyvan kit has a lot of wood in it! All pieces are precut and sanded to shape. Each part is numbered in the order it'll be needed for building. (Photo by Jennifer Pratt)

sheets on my workshop walls (and window) and went through the construction thoroughly. Eventually I developed a good working concept of the machine. Doubt soon gave way to enthusiasm.

Cambria kits come with hand-sawn and sanded parts. Each one is numbered. I laid them out in piles of ten, all the 30s and 50s and 90s together. This made life a lot easier as construction progressed.

The first step is to assemble the plywood frames that make up the core of the fuselage box. This will give you an introduction to the Cambria plans, which are dead accurate and very detailed. The numbering system for parts is a Godsend, and any wood stock that isn't numbered is always shown on the plan.

I was a bit surprised, since all the wooden pieces are preshaped, that I had to form the landing gear straps out of small strips of steel. But it turned out to be simple. I bent them around the gear with a pair of slip-joint pliers, and trimmed them off where necessary with a HOB Tuf-Grind. The soft metal is easily drilled with an Ace Handrill.

Fuselage Sides

The instructions say to sheet the fuselage sides before joining them with the cross braces, to keep the framework rigid. I applied my Schoolyard Scale experience and framed the whole basic box before sheeting. I had no problems at all with this method. It's a fairly complex structure, with lots of ¼ square longerons in the corners. Use a triangle to keep everything straight, and you'll wind up with a sturdy box that's a lot lighter than slab sides would be.

Nose Section

The nose section is built around the crutch that supports the nose gear. This gives you a very nice ''firewall'' to build a steerable nose gear against. It seems that the Europeans don't consider steerable nosewheels a necessity, but in a plane as complex as the Skyvan, what's one more subsystem?

I installed a Goldberg steerable nosewheel strut and bracket. The nosewheel requires its own servo, connected to the rudder channel with a Y-connector.

The plywood formers that bear most of the weight are precut, and ply doublers glue over the corners. The sides fit into precut slots in the formers. (Photo by Jennifer Pratt)

The side formers and bottom formers of the nose section are formed to the shape needed to match the molded nose cone and windshield. I tack-glued the whole assembly together to get a clearer idea of how it has to fit. Then I trimmed the nose cone and trial fitted it. A little sanding and trimming, and I was ready to screw the nose cone in place with the preshaped hardwood pieces. Once I had it in place and straight, I shaped the side pieces to conform to the nose cone and sheeted the sides with ⅛ sheet, grain vertical. A coarse belt on the Wedge Lock, a little elbow grease, and I had the shape right. Model Magic Filler rounded out the joints between the vertical side sheets. I couldn't resist taking a break to admire it, since this was the first time the Skyvan looked like an airplane, and not the box an airplane comes in!

Wings

The wing ribs are all stack-sanded at the fac-

tory. All that's necessary is to drill them for the various pushrods. I used two ¼ square spars to hold the balsa ribs square for drilling. Drill the balsa ribs a few at a time. Check the locations of the wing

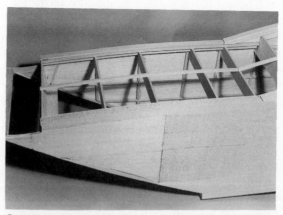

Once the sides are connected and sheeted, corner pieces are installed and sanded to shape. (Photo by Jennifer Pratt)

When the fuselage is sheeted and the corners are sanded round, the joints and seams can be filled in and sanded smooth. There's a lot of sanding to be done; a sanding block makes it easier. (Photo by Jennifer Pratt)

mounting blocks (inside the first two ribs on each wing) to make sure they don't block the holes. Note that you don't have to drill *all* the balsa ribs for the pushrods. The only hole that has to go through all the ribs is the one for the tip light wiring.

To accommodate this wiring for the McDaniel nav lights and wingtip strobes, I drilled another hole through the ribs near the high point of the ribs, forward of the spars. This will keep the wiring from interfering with the pushrods for flaps and ailerons.

The 1/16 ply used for spar webbing in the inner wing structure (the hardwood ribs) is cut from four unmarked strips of ply. I used one of these as a handy straightedge to slice up a lot of scrap 1/16 sheet balsa into spar webbing for the outer wing. Don't overlook the fact that the inner structure has ply webbing on *both* sides of the spars!

McDaniel Lighting System

The lighting system I picked is the one from

The ribs must be drilled to allow the pushrods for ailerons and flaps to come through. Each has a bellcrank mounted on a ply platform. The center ply platform is for attaching the strut. (Photo by Jennifer Pratt)

McDaniel RC Service. It allows you to use one channel to sequentially activate running lights, wingtip strobes, and landing lights. The electronic switcher that does this allows you to select whether you want nav lights that blink (military style) or lights that brighten and dim. The system comes with a pack of five 1200 mAh ni-cad cells for power, so there is very little drain from the receiver battery; the switcher draws less current than a servo would. There's also a slow charger for the battery pack.

Since you can set the point in the control throw where the lights come on, you can use a switched channel to activate the McDaniel lighting system. I decided to use a proportional channel instead, since I had one handy on the face of my Multiplex transmitter.

The connector wiring is simple, and the connectors you'd need for an ordinary installation are included. The Skyvan isn't an ordinary installation, since the wings are two separate panels. You'll need three connectors for each wing to wire in the tip strobes, landing lights, and nav lights. I used Deans connectors from Ace RC.

I installed the battery pack in the nose, right behind the nosewheel servo, since the plane needed some nose weight. I installed the charge jack in the radio floor. Then I used servo tape to put the electronic switcher out of the way on the underside of the roof. Once you have it set where you want it, you won't need access to it anymore, and the radio floor is already crowded!

I glued the strobe circuit boards into the wings near the wingtips, and ran short leads through holes in the balsa wingtip blocks to the strobe tubes. Af-

The McDaniel Lighting System controls the navigation lights, landing lights, and wingtip strobes. They can be turned on and off sequentially from the transmitter. The battery pack was mounted in the nose of the Skyvan, and the charging jack in the radio floor. (Photo by Jennifer Pratt)

ter the plane was painted, I glued the tubes to the wingtip with silicone sealer. They need to be held firmly in place. They get plenty of protection tucked up under the ply tip plates.

The nav light sockets were fitted into holes drilled in the front of each wingtip block. I trimmed the rubber grommets off the colored lenses supplied with the lights, exposing the threads underneath. Then I made sockets for the lenses by giving the threads a light coat of Vaseline, putting them in place, and filling around them with Model Magic. When the Model Magic hardened, I unscrewed the lenses.

The landing lights are located where the strut attaches to the underside of the wing. The kit includes a piece of plywood cut in a teardrop shape to serve as a base for the fillet at this point. I attached the piece to the metal strut fitting, drilled a small hole in the back of it for the light wire, and glued the reflector in position. Then I coated the wire and bulb with Vaseline and inserted them in the reflector, routing the wire up through the hole. I cut a short piece of 3/16 diameter brass tubing and glued it in place around the attachment bolt head. Finally, I filled in around the whole business with Model Magic. It took three applications of the filler to get

The wings are supported on top by bolts that go through steel straps anchored inside the fuselage, and hardwood blocks in the wing. Each wing is supported from underneath by the wing strut. (Photo by Jennifer Pratt)

the shape I wanted. Since the wire didn't stick to the filler, I can pull the bulb out far enough to replace it if need be.

Since the strut has to be removable, another connector is called for. I used Deans pins again, cutting a hole in the wing sheeting big enough to stuff them inside before attaching the strut. The fairing covers the hole nicely.

There are four connectors that have to come into the radio area from each wing panel: nav light, strobe power, landing light, and strobe sync. A slot cut between the holes in the fuselage that admit the aileron and flap pushrod makes it a lot easier to stuff all this wiring into the fuse. Ace Spiral Wrap is an enormous help to keep the wiring straight. It's a thick strip of plastic that sets in a spiral, and wraps around the bundle of wires, holding them together.

I glued the female connectors from the light controller to one of the plywood struts in the radio bay, facing up. The leads from the wing panels plug vertically into these. Dabs of paint color-code the plugs, so you don't wind up plugging the landing lights into the strobe circuit. Not that this hurts anything; I did it several times in the process of working all this out.

Engine Nacelles

When you build the engine nacelles, the plans are going to be more helpful to you than the instructions. But once you trial-fit some of the machined pieces together, you'll have no trouble at all. The main plywood former for each nacelle is split at the top. This gives you some leeway to allow a good fit between the wing ribs. I fitted the vertical ply sides to the former, then plugged them into the wing bay. The fit was good, so I tack-glued the whole assembly in place and used the large balsa side and rear pieces to round out the nacelle. Several of the pieces are deliberately oversize, so you should plan to remove the nacelle assembly from the wing for shaping before permanently gluing it into the wing rib bay.

The plans show where to cut a hole in the rear of the nacelle to simulate the turbine exhaust port. I chose to cut this hole all the way through, so I could look at the fuel tank without removing the engine mount.

The plans call for a 6-ounce square tank in each nacelle, and that's just what there's room for! I made fitting the Sullivan 6-ounce square tanks I used a little easier by routing the rear nacelle pieces until they fit over the lower rear edge of the tank. It was a simple matter of enlarging the inner side of the hole I'd already cut. When you make up the tank stopper, plan for the tank to be resting on its side, and point both the fuel and vent lines straight down. They don't have to be very long.

The nylon engine mounts supplied with the kit fit the Enya .46 four-stroke engines beautifully. I used self-tapping screws into small pilot holes to attach the engines to the mounts, and similar screws to attach the mounts to the firewalls. You have to be careful not to use screws that are too long; each firewall has to fit flush against the main former of its nacelle. They must also be removable to allow access to the tank; I accomplished this with longer self-tapping screws screwed through the firewalls into the formers.

Throttle Linkages

Once the engine is in place, you can route the throttle pushrod. The kit includes cables for throttle linkages, and calls for you to solder an L-shaped piece of music wire to the end of a length of the cable for the throttle linkage. The cable is called for because of the tight bend the throttle linkage has to go through just inside the wing behind the engine.

Because of my lousy soldering technique, I decided to try flexible plastic pushrods instead of cable. The yellow Sullivan rods will work, but just barely. I installed Sullivan rod on one side and it went around the corner nicely. But it still wasn't as free as I would have liked it.

Then I noticed a new product from Standale Aircraft Company just for this purpose. It's a thin, solid nylon rod running in an outer sleeve tube about the diameter of the inner Sullivan rod. You can tie this stuff in a knot and it'll still be perfectly free. I bought two lengths and ran one through the outer Sullivan tube I already had installed. It fit beautifully.

The only thing that gave me any trouble at all with the Standale pushrod is the fact that the only way to attach the control surface to it is with the

The engines nacelles are made of precut ply pieces that glue to ply ribs. The two firewall pieces are held together with screws. Unscrewing them allows access to the fuel tank, which sits right behind the engine. (Photo by Jennifer Pratt)

supplied connector. The throttle arm on the Enyas is pretty close to the back of the case. Since the pushrod exits on the outside of the engine mount, the easiest way to connect the rod to the throttle arm would be with a piece of metal rod bent 90 degrees and projecting through the throttle arm. Fortunately, the Standale pushrod is so flexible that it accommodated the slight bend necessary to connect with the throttle arm very well. I reoriented the throttle arm so that it gives full throttle at the six o'clock position and is pulled back to idle at three o'clock.

The Standale rod has to be supported through almost its entire length because it's so flexible, so it was necessary to glue part of the outer tube into position inside the fuselage next to the servo. I mounted a small block of balsa under the wing mounting tab attachments, and glued the outer tube to it, next to the servo. Then I unbolted the wing, removed the inner rod, and sawed through the outer rod between the wing and the fuselage. This leaves you with a length of inner pushrod projecting from the root of the wing. It turned out to be a very smooth installation, and I'm completely satisfied with it.

Glow Plug Connection

The only fault I've ever found with the Enya .46

is the fact that the glow plug is at the front of the engine. This is no problem if you use a remote glow plug connector, as you're supposed to. But the temptation is there to slip a glow plug connector on the plug. I've done it and gotten away with it, but I've also gotten my knuckles rapped on the backside of a whirling prop! One lesson like that was enough, and I now put a Remote Headlock or similar device on all of my four-stroke engines that have forward-facing plugs.

I decided to install an onboard glow heat system in the Skyvan, since it certainly had room for another battery. I used a system from McDaniel RC Service that has a D-cell ni-cad battery for power. This was simple to install, but it meant two more wires coming out of each wing that have to be connected to plugs inside the fuselage! I secured the battery in the nose of the plane, then mounted the plugs for connecting to the wing leads in the forward wall of the radio bay. These plugs also allow me to charge the battery.

Plastic Cowl

Once all this is done, you can start work on the plastic cowling pieces. These are quite easy to work with if you don't rush the job. Trim the flash off each cowl half as shown, and test-fit them together. The plastic edges can be sanded with your sanding block to straighten them up. Once the edges match, cut the clearance for the engine in the bottom by trying each half on the nacelle and cutting away a bit more each time. Don't worry about making a tight fit; you want plenty of clearance around the head of the engine to allow air to exit.

When it all fits, glue the halves together with a thin bead of cement on the edge of one cowl half. I like to use Plastic-Zap for applications like this, but Super Jet works fine, too. The instructions recommend reinforcing the glue joints with strips of scrap plastic on the inside.

Once you have the cowl halves together, cut the air inlet in the front of the cowl below the engine shaft. Trim it until the edges are even.

The kit includes soft balsa blocks to fill in between the back of the engine nacelle and the top surface of the wing. I used them for the deepest part,

and made a nice fairing with Model Magic.

Wing Sheeting

Now you're ready to sheet the wing, install the leading edge, and smooth the whole business. I have two tips that make this process a lot easier for me. First, I use Super Jet for everything, and I deal with the ridge of glue along the joints by wet-sanding with Debonder. Second, I use Model Magic Filler a lot, but before I put it on, I whip plenty of air into it. Mixing it thoroughly makes it lighter and doesn't affect its adhesion.

I cut holes in a piece of wing sheeting to clear the flap pushrod and glued it in place from the tip inward. Then I fitted another long sheet forward of this one to the leading edge. Finally, I filled in the sheeting to the wing root, cutting slots to clear the wing mounting tabs. Make sure the grain of the sheeting is running parallel to the leading edge!

Finishing

I finished the Skyvan with fiberglass cloth, using K&B Clear Epoxy Paint to adhere it. The technique is described in detail in Chapter 5 of *The Beginner's Guide to Radio Control Sport Flying*, (TAB Book No. 3020). Lightweight cloth makes it easy.

After applying a second coat of K&B Clear and sanding it, I sprayed on two coats of K&B Gloss

A lot of servos have to fit in the radio compartment! There's a servo for each aileron, one for the elevator, one for the rudders, and one for the cargo door. (Photo by Jennifer Pratt)

White. This gave me a nice smooth finish with minimal effort.

Flying

I wanted a good-sized field to test fly the Skyvan, so I visited a field in nearby Maryland. I tested everything, after having a couple of expert friends look everything over. Then I spent about half an hour taxiing around and running up the engines.

When I was satisfied, it was moment-of-truth time.

The Skyvan had no surprises in store for me. Climbout was fine, control was positive, and the approaches with the flaps partway down were a joy to see. I'm not about to try any aerobatics; the plane isn't designed for it. But the flaps open up some very interesting possibilities for different flight speeds. I'm enjoying the learning process. Meanwhile, I have one plane that I'm certain will attract a lot of interest at a busy flying field!

Chapter 7

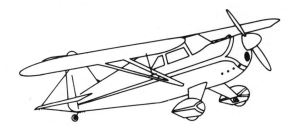

Ducted Fan Aircraft

IT'S A QUESTION THAT'S ALWAYS ASKED: "HOW DO you fly an RC jet model?" Everyone sees jets constantly at airports and on television; propeller-driven airplanes are almost an endangered species. Thanks to the movies, it's getting so people recognize the F-15s and F-16s before the Piper Cubs.

People are sometimes disappointed when you tell them that there are no true jet engines small enough to stuff into one of our models. There are pulse jets that have been used for years in Control Line Speed competition. They are cantankerous beasts, loud enough to wake the dead, requiring special fuel mixtures and pressurization to start. And once they're going, if you don't get them into the air right away so they can cool off, they have the charming habit of getting red hot and sometimes setting the model on fire. Furthermore, they aren't throttleable; they're either going full blast, or dead. But after their run they don't always *stay* dead, "blurping" to momentary life a time or two. This can really foul up your approach! I really don't recommend using a pulse jet in an RC model. It's difficult, it could be dangerous, and there are better

ways to do the same thing.

A team in Britain actually designed and constructed a tiny gas turbine engine and flew it in a radio-controlled model. From the reports I read in the British model magazines, the project was very successful. The engine was fully throttleable, and several models were built and flown for it. But the investment in building the engine was very high as well, and I really don't expect the gas turbine to appear on the market any time soon.

So what's the practical alternative? Ducted fans. A ducted fan is a powerplant consisting of a conventional model engine enclosed in a tube. The engine drives a multi-bladed fan. The tube supports the engine and usually several *stators*, or static blades, to align the airflow through the tube. The engine pulls air through the tube and exhausts it out the back to produce thrust.

If it sounds inefficient, well, it's not as efficient as a conventional propeller. But the modern ducted fan units available today will produce plenty of power for a typical model. Like electric power, ducted fan technology is just coming into its own. The ducted

This unusual ducted fan plane is the Jetster, designed by Dick Sarpolus, who has written an excellent book on fan flying. I can't imagine a better training fan plane; the engine is right there where you can work on it, and flight characteristics are excellent. (Photo courtesy *Model Retailer* magazine)

fan kits available today are not marginal designs, and while they're not recommended for rank beginners, anyone with reasonable modeling skills will have no trouble producing a good working jet model.

ENGINES

Ducted fans require engines that will turn high rpm. Since the engine is completely enclosed by the fan unit, it isn't going to get the same kind of cooling airflow that a regular engine will. These requirements call for some special engines.

K&B was one of the first to come out with a fan engine, and their 7.5cc fan engine is still a standard. Rossi has developed several very powerful fan engines: a .61, a .65, and an .81. The O.S. .77 features a special carburetor that is very easy to tune,

plus a large cooling head.

The engine you select depends very much on the fan unit you will use. Since engines are such a tight fit within the fans, the fan units are usually designed around a particular engine. A tuned pipe is usually required, and that also influences engine selection. Read the fan unit instructions for their recommendations. In the case of the Byro-Jet unit from Byron Originals, you can order units for several different engines, drilled and tapped to fit.

FLYING TECHNIQUES

Flying a ducted fan model is no more difficult than flying a conventional airplane. The same things govern the flight. Is the center of gravity in the right place? Is the engine running properly? Use your ex-

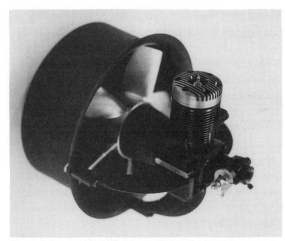

Several companies make ducted fan units for different sizes of engines. Most fan kits are designed for one or another of these units; it's best to stick with the unit recommended by the manufacturer. This is the Byro-Jet, made by Byron Originals. (Photo courtesy Byron Originals)

strip, make sure the grass is short and the ground is smooth.

Once you're in the air, you can start to enjoy yourself. About the only caution I can think of is to keep the speed up. Visualize the airflow through the model. It's possible to put the plane in attitudes where air can't get into the plane at all—vertical stalls, obviously, but there are others. Holding the nose high in slow flight will dramatically decrease the airflow. Sometimes this can lead to engine cooling problems.

Airspeed is the most crucial thing to keep in mind. Landings should be fast, using the throttle more than the elevator. If the engine quits, get the nose down and keep your speed up as long as you can. Don't try to stretch the glide to make it to the field. A ''full-size'' flying instructor I know once told me, ''If you have to land, pretend there's a runway underneath you, and land on it.''

perience with conventional planes to set up your fan ship properly.

Generally speaking, hard surface runways are preferable. Ducted fan models pull air in the front, which makes them very effective vacuum cleaners as they move down the runway. Sweeping the runway is a good idea. If you *must* take off from a grass

TWO POPULAR DUCTED FAN KITS

Bob Violett Sport Shark. One ducted fan kit that has made a large impact on the RC scene in recent years is the Sport Shark from Bob Violett Models. It's a series of kits, all based around the

This is one version of the Sport Shark, an excellent sport fan kit from Bob Violett Models. The Spot Shark is largely prefabricated with lightweight carbon fiber composites. Performance is sparkling, making the Sport Shark an excellent first ducted fan kit. (Photo courtesy Bob Violett Models)

same basic fuselage, power unit and dimensions. You can get a Sport Shark kit with a swept vertical fin, or a more standard clipped-delta shape. The newest version is called the Aggressor, and it looks for all the world like an F-5 or F-20 military jet.

Violett kits are special for several reasons. One of the biggest reasons for their excellent performance is light weight. This is accomplished by careful designing, excellent fiberglass work, and liberal use of Violett's "Magnalite" carbon fiber composite material. This workmanship, combined with the advanced design of the entire airplane-powerplant system, gives you a ducted fan plane with an amazingly wide speed range. It can slow down beautifully for landings, with or without the optional flaps down. On a trimmed grass field, a rollout of 80 feet or so will have you in the air.

The Sport Shark kits are highly prefabbed, but will still take you about three weeks of evenings to put together. You get prebuilt wings, stabilizer, and fin. These can be covered with iron-on film or very lightweight fiberglass cloth. The pushrods, bellcranks, and retract mounts are installed in the wing at the factory. The fuselage, top hatch, nose gear hatch, tailpipe, and inlets are high-quality fiberglass. You even get Magnalite material for servo trays and

nose gear mounting. This kit is well worth its price.

Byron Originals F-16. Byron Originals has earned a unique reputation for turning out high-quality kits with a great deal of prefabrication. You never quite know what they're going to release next; the range goes from the sublime SeaWind amphibian to the ridiculous Pipe Dream sport airplane.

Byron is noted for ducted fan kits; they have been one of the leaders in the field since they began. Their ByroJet power system was designed for their kits, and they have a series of engine mounts and tuned pipes to fit it. Their kits feature extensive use of fiberglass and foam, all engineered for minimum weight.

One of their most popular kits is a scale model of the F-16 Fighting Falcon jet fighter. It's pretty typical of Byron kit construction, so I took a closer look at it. The obvious reason for its popularity is its looks, but the flyability has a lot to do with it, too. Most ducted fan models need a hard surface runway and plenty of room to get off. The F-16 gets off the ground quickly, and can be flown easily from grass runways.

The F-16 fuselage is fiberglass, molded in two pieces: the main fuselage and a nose cone. They're indexed so that it's impossible to misalign them when

The Byron F-16 is a very popular fan kit. Who can resist these good looks? The wingtip rockets and drop tanks are optional; so is a custom set of retractable landing gear. (Photo courtesy Byron Originals)

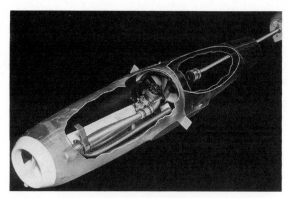

Ducted fan units are started with a standard electric starter, such as the ones made by Sullivan. Some use a belt that engages a pulley on the engine shaft; others use an extension that reaches in through the tailpipe. (Photo courtesy Byron Originals)

you're gluing them together. The wings are molded foam, with a hard surface. Byron recommends covering them with a low-temperature film. I've been very successful with Black Baron Film directly over bare foam. Do as the instructions say, however, and be certain of your iron temperature before you start.

Test-fitting all components that go into the fuselage before gluing them in place is a good idea. As with any ducted fan aircraft, be sure that the center of gravity is where the plans say it ought to be.

Your engine needs to be well-broken-in and putting out the thrust it's capable of before you fly. Break in the engine on a test stand with a prop. Install it in the plane, and run it up to check the installation. Now measure the thrust with a spring scale. You should be getting around 10 pounds of thrust

from the Byro-Jet unit and the recommended O.S. engine or the special K&B 7.5cc fan engine.

The Byro-Jet has its engine in a ''pusher'' arrangement, which puts it in a good position to work on. You order a Byro-Fan predrilled to fit the engine you plan to use. The special Byro-Jet tuned pipe has to be used; it fits neatly within the F-16's scale air scoop.

The battery and receiver fit easily in the nose. The F-16's fuselage is big, so equipment installation is no problem. Don't deviate from the kit instructions; they have everything carefully worked out.

Fuel tank installation is a bit unusual. To guarantee good fuel flow in any position, a twin tank setup is used. The tanks are connected with a pipe that runs through the mating surface between the two. The larger tank feeds the smaller tank in such a way that the smaller tank has the same level of fuel in it most of the time. Since the smaller tank is mounted level with the carburetor, this greatly improves the engine runs.

The best way to start the engine is with the extension shaft that Byron sells. It fits standard Sullivan starters and reaches in the tailpipe to engage the nut on the engine shaft.

Flying the F-16 is a pleasant experience. Since there's no propwash over the air surfaces, you have to expect the controls to get a little mushy at low speeds. Landing involves use of the throttle to keep the speed up. If you have a flameout, point the nose down and maintain speed as you're lining up with the end of the runway. Don't try to extend the glide by holding the nose high, or your landing will look like a pancake landing on a skillet.

Chapter 8

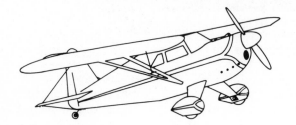

Helicopters

RC HELICOPTERS ARE GAINING VERY RAPIDLY IN popularity. They're a relatively new thing in the RC world; practical helicopter kits have only been on the market for the last decade or so. Now there is a very wide range of products available for helicopter enthusiasts, and more are coming all the time. You'll find plenty of special radios, engines, mufflers, fuels, and accessories for helicopters.

Most model magazines have regular helicopter columns. These are gold mines of good information on new products, flying techniques, and modification tips. I've gotten a lot of help from the ''Chopper Chatter'' column in *Model Builder* magazine. *RC Modeler* also runs an excellent helicopter column. Serious chopper fliers should catch these every month.

WHERE TO BEGIN

The most important thing a beginning helicopter flier can do is get expert help. It's possible to teach yourself to fly helicopters, but you're very likely to use up a machine or two in the process—

not to mention your time, money, and blood pressure. RC helicopters are not easy to fly. If you can find someone else to check your construction, help you get it balanced and adjusted, and coach you through the first flights, you'll be way ahead of the game.

Your hobby shop is the first place to look for an expert. Often the store has an employee or two who will give you a lot of help. If not, they can steer you to the next place to look, your local flying club. If you're not near a hobby shop and can't find a club, write or call the AMA for a list of clubs in your area. Find the closest club, and attend a meeting with your machine. You're almost certain to find someone who can help you out. It's well worth the trouble, since it can help you make your helicopter live longer.

There are several excellent beginner-level helicopters on the market. All of these feature a large amount of preassembly of the drivetrain, the ability to accept different brands of motors, fully detailed instructions, and a good supply of spare parts. Look for these features in *any* helicopter kit you buy.

Schlueter mechanics can be easily installed in a wide range of scale fuselages. This Bell Long Ranger is one example. (Photo courtesy *Model Retailer* magazine)

The Hirobo Shuttle has done more to bring new-comers into RC helicopters than any other product. There's a very simple reason for this: The Shuttle comes fully assembled. You can buy a Shuttle that needs only the installation of an engine and radio, or one that has the engine and radio in it. Some specialist hobby shops will sell you a Shuttle that not only has everything installed, but has been adjusted and tested by an expert. This gives the beginner a machine that he is absolutely confident will fly. No wonder it has been so successful.

The Shuttle is a nice, stable, solid machine, but it is relatively small. Larger helicopters with .40 to .60 engines are often recommended for beginners, since they have more available power and are generally more stable than smaller machines. For those who prefer to build, or who prefer a larger machine than the Shuttle, there are several alternatives. Schlueter's Mini-Boy .40-size helicopter and Heli-Star, Champion, and Superior .60 machines have taught a lot of people to fly. The Champion and Superior are relatively expensive, but they can be bought with basic mechanics for flight training and upgraded to competitive machines later. Both are outstanding helicopters.

Gorham's Cricket was the standard trainer machine until the Shuttle came along. It's still good for the purpose, but there are better ones. Gorham's Cobra is a larger, more stable machine than the Cricket, and is in my opinion a better training machine. It can be hopped up later for advanced competition.

Kavan's Jet Ranger is a classic machine that has

The Gorham Cricket is a small, relatively simple machine that has taught hundreds of helicopter pilots to fly. It's still a good choice, although more modern machines can be better. (Photo courtesy *Model Retailer* magazine)

been very popular. It's a large, stable helicopter that's sold for a very reasonable price. The smaller Kavan Shark 40 is also a good training machine at a lower price. The Shark is available with or without collective pitch control; I strongly recommend getting the collective.

HELICOPTER RADIOS

You understand that you need a helicopter radio, but why *exactly* do you need one? What are all these special functions for, and which ones should you look for when you buy your radio system?

To answer that, let's take a look at the features you can find on a modern heli radio, one by one, and describe each one's usefulness. Then when you go to your hobby shop to look for a heli radio, you'll know what to ask about and why.

Throttle-Collective Mixing

In simple terms, the throttle makes your heli go up and down. If you have a fixed-pitch machine,

that's the extent of it. However, a machine with *collective pitch* requires that you mix the pitch and the throttle for smooth vertical flight. Collective pitch, remember, is the pitch angle of the blades, something like the pitch angle of a propeller. The angle is the same for both blades. The higher this pitch angle, the more lift generated by the rotor. (Don't confuse this with *cyclic pitch*, which is the change in pitch of an individual rotor blade to bank the machine in an aileron-like effect.)

Throttle-collective mixing puts both the throttle and collective pitch control on the same stick—namely, the throttle stick. So, as you increase the throttle from idle, you can increase the pitch angle of the rotor blades to give you more lift. All this happens without you having to think about it.

Now, you could accomplish this by using a Y-cable to plug both the throttle and collective servo into the throttle channel on the receiver. You could even hook the throttle and collective pushrods up to different holes on the same servo output arm, and run them both from one servo. But there are a lot

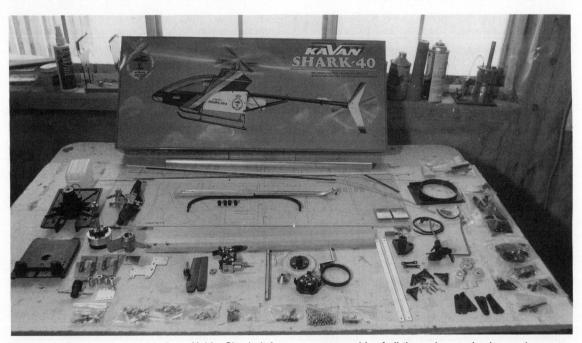

The Kavan Shark 40 is available from Hobby Shack. It features preassembly of all the major mechanics, such as rotor head and autorotation clutch. Small parts are in numbered bags to ease assembly. Popular .40 to .45 size engines will fit the Shark. (Photo by Jennifer Pratt)

Gorham Cobra and Competitor mechanics can be built into many scale fuselages for competition or just for good looks. This Jet Ranger is an excellent example. (Photo courtesy *Model Retailer* magazine)

of advantages to having a transmitter that allows you to mix the two, and having throttle and collective on two separate channels. First and foremost, it makes it a heck of a lot easier to set up your machine. Second, once you're set up, you can trim these two functions independently. Finally, it allows you to deal with something called the *pitch-throttle curve*.

The pitch-throttle curve comes about because the optimum relationship between throttle and pitch position is not linear. Huh? Well, suppose the ideal pitch for your machine with the throttle full open is, say, 8 degrees. At idle, the best pitch angle is negative 2 degrees. (The angle should be negative at idle to hold the machine on the ground; pitch will increase when you add throttle to take off.) If pitch and throttle are mixed in a straight-line fashion, at half throttle you get 3 degrees of pitch. Half throttle is where a heli should hover, and you really need about 5 degrees of collective pitch for a good hover. So, we need to add more collective pitch in the throttle range from idle to half than we add in the range from half to full. When you diagram this relationship (remember your high school algebra, which you thought you'd never use?), it comes out as a curve;

hence the term "throttle-pitch curve."

With the throttle and the collective pitch on two separate channels, a smart transmitter can give you an adjustment to hit this curve just right. You do it by setting the endpoint of your collective channel. In the above example, if we set the endpoints of the collective servo at pitches of −2 degrees on the low end and 12 degrees on the high end, we get our midpoint of 5 degrees. Since endpoint adjustment doesn't stop the pitch abruptly, it evens out into a smooth curve over the range of mixing.

All heli radios have throttle-collective mixing. They do not necessarily have endpoint adjustment on the collective channel, though. Look for it.

Throttle-Tail Rotor Mixing

There are two different types of mixing functions that combine the throttle and the tail rotor. The first of these, *acceleration*, is used only on fixed-pitch helicopters. Acceleration mixing gives a brief blast of tail rotor power when the throttle is advanced, and quickly returns to normal. This counters the torque from the faster-turning rotor. It's similar to what you have to do with most fixed-wing airplanes when you have to hold some rudder to keep the plane tracking straight as you increase throttle.

Collective pitch machines use the second type of throttle-tail rotor mixing, *revolution mixing*. As the throttle stick is advanced, the pitch of the tail rotor advances to counter the increased torque of the rotor. This is a smooth, linear motion.

Once again, all heli radios have this feature. It's really most useful in hovering flight to help you keep your orientation while lifting off and hovering. When you're in motion, the gyro does most of the work necessary to maintain your heading and keep the tail where it is until you tell it to move.

High Idle or Idle-Up

When you have the throttle and collective pitch on different channels, some radios will allow you to set an adjustment called *high idle* (or *idle-up*). When you switch this function on, your throttle operates normally from full open down to the position you set (usually the amount of throttle you need to hover). When you pull back the stick to this point, the throttle holds steady but the collective pitch continues to be controllable. You can use this feature to main-

tain a constant rotor rpm, controlling your ascent and descent almost entirely with the collective pitch. This is pretty much the way full-scale helicopters fly!

If you're into aerobatics, you can set the high idle point higher than hover, so you can actually get a little negative collective pitch while maintaining full rotor speed. This is very useful in maneuvers that call for you to be inverted briefly, such as loops and axial rolls.

Throttle Hold

A function similar to idle-up is *throttle hold*. When you throw this switch, the throttle is held at a predetermined setting. Unlike high idle, where the throttle still operates above the set point, with throttle hold there is no movement at all. The main use for this function is to practice autorotations. You can set the throttle hold point to idle, and reduce the engine to idle while maintaining full cyclic pitch control, then get the rotor speed back up by switching the engine back in.

Be very careful that you don't have your throttle hold set at a high rpm. If you hit the switch accidentally, before or during starting, the engine

Gorham Model Products sell Hirobo helis. Several well-detailed scale fuselages are available for Hirobo mechanics; this turbine-powered Japanese machine is an impressive example. (Photo courtesy *Model Retailer* magazine)

would go to full speed immediately and you could have a serious accident! That's another good reason why you should always hold the rotor head firmly while starting the engine.

Hovering Throttle

Hovering throttle is really a trim function. It allows you to make fine throttle adjustments when the throttle stick is halfway up, the ideal hovering position. Depending on how heavy your machine is (and other factors), it will like to hover best at slightly different rotor speeds. The hovering throttle adjustment will allow you to set this speed without affecting the other functions on the throttle stick.

Invert Switch

Many advanced heli radios have an inverted flight switch. This flips your collective pitch control to the opposite of its normal pitch to give you negative pitch for sustained inverted flight without affecting the throttle function. Frankly, I don't care for this function very much. Inverted flight isn't something to try on your first machine, or even your second, unless you have expert help. Having the switch there means it could be hit accidentally. If this happens in flight, you will be unceremoniously dumped onto the ground. If it happens before flight, you could stand there wondering why the heli is plastered to the earth. Some systems allow you to unplug the switch internally or disable it in some other way. Others have a guard over it. Whatever safety feature you have, be aware of that invert switch. You won't need it for a while, and it can bite you if you don't handle it carefully.

ENGINES

Several manufacturers have come out with special engines for helicopters. The difference between a heli engine and a standard one is often just the shape of the head. Since engines in helicopters don't get air flowing over them at high speeds, larger fins are put on the head to improve cooling. Most modern helicopters incorporate a turbine-type fan that fits onto the driveshaft and directs cooling air over the engine.

In fact, the large cooling fins on heli engines aren't absolutely necessary in most cases. Thanks to cooling fans—and the fact that heli engines are seldom run at full throttle—overheating engines hasn't been a problem. An exception to this is scale helicopters, where the engine is sometimes hidden completely underneath the scale body. But in most cases, you can install just about any standard aircraft engine that fits in your helicopter.

Several heli engines are worthy of special note. Enya's special helicopter engine incorporates an innovative throttle design that greatly improves the throttle response at midrange. Webra makes a special engine for the popular Shuttle ready-built helicopter. There's a special Magnum engine for helicopters; the Magnum line is available from Hobby Shack. Engine mounts and mufflers designed for O.S. engines will also fit Magnums.

You should select an engine to fit your particular helicopter, not the other way around. Some helicopters will require a special header pipe from the exhaust port of the engine to allow you to hook up the muffler. Often there's no room for a stand-

The Enya SS30H is typical of small helicopter engines. It has a large heat sink on the head to assist cooling in the relatively quiet air inside a helicopter fuselage. The Enya also has a special carburetor to improve throttle response. Several companies make special helicopter mufflers to fit the Enya engines. (Photo courtesy Altech Marketing)

ard airplane-type muffler. Fortunately, there are a whole bunch of special helicopter mufflers available. Looking at the plans for your helicopter will tell you whether you need one of these or not.

GYROS

I'm sure that most of the helicopters flying in this country today have a gyro on board. The gyro is a small device that connects to the receiver; the tail rotor plugs into it. It runs from the receiver battery. Since a gyro has a small electric motor in it, it soaks up some power. Most kits recommend that you use a larger battery pack for the receiver if you use a gyro.

The gyro is simply a device that tells the tail to stay where it is. When the speed of the main rotor changes, the change in centrifugal force moves the tail. Mechanically linking the tail rotor with the main rotor will help control this movement, but the ideal way to control it is with a device that senses the force and adjusts the tail rotor accordingly. That's a gyro.

Most major radio system manufacturers make a gyro to fit their radios. Futaba and JR offer different models. Gorham took over production of the popular Kraft gyro when Kraft went out of the RC business. Beemer RC imports the Multiplex gyro for their radios.

Should you buy a gyro? *Absolutely*. Flying helicopters is difficult enough; anything that makes it easier means that you can devote more of your energy to enjoying it. For the extra $60 to $100 that it will add to the cost of your helicopter, it's well worth it.

HELICOPTER BLADES

The blades of your helicopter are probably the most important part, since they're both wings *and* propeller. They're also the parts that are most subject to crash damage. When an inexperienced heli pilot gets into trouble, the blades are the first things to go. When I bought my first helicopter, I followed the advice of a knowledgeable friend and bought two extra sets of blades on the spot.

If you want to buy spare blades, a logical place to start is the manufacturer of your heli kit. They

know best what's required for their machine. However, there are now some companies that specialize in replacement blades for all the popular helicopter models. Sometimes these will be more expensive than original equipment—and there are usually good reasons for it.

I've been experimenting with some blades from Yale Manufacturing, who produce the "Tru-Spin" brand of blades. These blades are really very complex. They are formed from five laminations: the first three are hard maple, and the last two are a lighter wood. This puts the center of gravity slightly forward of the centerline of the blade, which is good. The Yale blades I tested were very consistent in their balance.

Yale blades come with blade holders that are contoured to match the blade, a nice touch. Glue these on with medium grade CyA, such as Super Jet, clamping the parts in place to make sure they're solid.

Balancing Rotor Blades

If you used heat-shrink tubing to cover your blades, here is a trick for balancing them that I picked up from Dick Grossman's column in *Model Builder* magazine. Weigh each blade on a sensitive gram scale. Cut a piece of heat-shrink tubing equal in weight to the difference in weight of the two blades. With the rotor blades on a High Point balancer, slide the tubing onto the light blade and move it back and forth until the blades are in balance. Use your heat gun to shrink it in place. Hey, presto—balanced blades!

Dick's column also provided this hint for doing a little field balancing. If you see a lot of shaking in the tail of your machine, your main blades could be out of balance. Wrap a rubber band around one of the blades several times. If the shaking gets worse, put the rubber band on the other blade. Move the band up and down the blade until the vibration is gone. When you get home, do a *proper* job of balancing the blades!

Weighting Rotor Blades

One of the competition tricks most often used with helis is to add weight to the blades. This increases the amount of momentum in each blade, and also has a stabilizing effect, since it makes the rotor disk a more efficient gyroscope. However, it's not something you attempt without knowing what you are doing!

There's some controversy in competition heli circles about using metal weights in rotor blades. This practice usually involves routing a slot in the underside of the blade and epoxying in lead pellets. It's not legal under AMA or FAI (international) rules to ballast blades with metal; the reason is safety. Suppose someone does a poor job of gluing the lead in place. When the rotor gets up to speed, if any of the lead leaves the blade, it's going to leave at high velocity—and there's no way of telling *where* it's going to go. I agree that this train of events is unlikely, but I prefer to err on the side of safety.

I've had a look at a product that solves the problem neatly. It's called Yaleweight, and it's sold by Yale Hobby Manufacturing, the people who make the Tru-Spin blades. Yaleweight is a thick epoxy-like paste. It's non-metallic, but still plenty heavy. You mix it up and squeegee it into slots routed in the underside of the blade. It sticks to the blade very well. Since it sets up softer than the maple of the blade, it can be easily sanded down to a perfect contour. If you want to weight your rotor blades, this is definitely the way to go.

Covering Rotor Blades

Once you have weight installed in your blades (if you choose to weight the blades), and you have the blade holders installed, you're ready to cover the blades. Some manufacturers tell you to cover the blade with a heat-shrink covering such as MonoKote. This works fine, and gives you a wide range of colors to choose from. Be certain, however, that you have *very* good adhesion of the covering all the way around the blade. If you have air trapped between the blade and the covering, centrifugal force will pull it toward the tip, loosening the covering as it goes. If the covering is loose, lift forces will try to pull it right off the blade. This distorts the lifting surface of the blade, making handling erratic. If some of the covering tears away completely, it can cause all sorts of unpleasant surprises.

A better solution to covering blades is the use of heat-shrink tubing. Several manufacturers supply this stuff with their blades, and I like it very much.

To cover a blade with heat-shrink tubing, first determine how much clearance you have between the wooden blade holder on the inside tip of each blade and the part of the rotor head that it clamps into. If it's a near fit, you may have to cut away the covering material over the blade holders. You want the blades to swing freely in the rotor head.

Some fliers I know give the blade a coat of clear polyurethane spray paint before covering. This fuel-proofs the blade and seals the wood grain.

Slide the covering down over the blade and shrink it with a heat gun or hair dryer. Start from the center and heat evenly all the way around the blade to prevent wrinkles. Leave some overhang at each end so you have something to hold the blade by. Shrink the covering down tight over each blade tip, then trim it off with a pair of scissors so that there's a little lip of covering left. Now put several drops of thin CyA on the tip, letting it soak into the wood. This seals the covering to the wood. Finally, using a sharp knife, trim the covering flush with the tip.

TRAINING GEAR

Before you fly your helicopter the first time, you should install a set of training gear. Training gear usually consists of two sturdy dowels with plastic balls at the tips. They're fastened together to form a cross and are attached firmly to the helicopter's landing gear. Several companies make training gear for their helis that can usually be adapted to other brands very quickly.

The main purpose of the training gear is to protect your blades. If you're hovering an inch or so above the ground and the machine starts to tip, the blades can strike the ground before you remember which way to move the sticks to level it out again. With those nice long dowels sticking out underneath, one of them will hit the ground before the rotor blades do. The result is an ungraceful belly-flop, but that's a lot better than pieces of rotor blade flying everywhere.

FLYING

Flying an RC helicopter is not unlike balancing yourself on top of a beach ball. It's a matter of feeling what's happening and responding to it. You'll be constantly correcting to get the motion that you want. Getting better is a matter of smoothing out these corrections until they're automatic.

The first time you fly your helicopter it might not even leave the ground. You should be feeling out the throttle response of the engine, seeing how much throttle it takes to make the machine light on its feet. While this is happening, watch the machine carefully for any signs of excessive vibration. When you spot problems, solve them before going any farther. The most you should do at this point is skid the model around a little bit on its gear.

After this first trial, go over the machine carefully. Look for components that have begun to loosen from vibration. Tighten everything. Reapply thread locking compounds if necessary. Loose parts are a double hazard: They create *more* vibration, and they can cause electrical interference. A helicopter with loose metal parts is a flying electrical storm.

As you get a good feel for the throttle, you should be able to get the machine almost to the point of lifting off. Practice holding it there and watch for any tendency to turn. Turning could indicate a problem with the trim on the tail rotor, or a poorly adjusted gyro.

Once you've gotten good at "hovering on the ground," start maneuvering the tail. Work slowly until you can swing the model around to point in any direction and hold it there. This is another good chance to get your gyro set up the way it should be.

Once you have learned how to put the tail where you want it, try gently skidding the machine forward. Work very slowly. You should be able to skid the machine forward, left, or right without ever lifting it off the training gear. Learning this now, rather than after you're at hovering height, will make things much easier. Hovering height is also crashing height!

When you can hold the model in any direction you choose, you can start actually lifting it off the ground. Concentrate on smoothness. Work until you can hold the model an inch or two off the ground— never farther than the length of the training gear.

Appendices

Appendix A

Radio Control Manufacturers and Suppliers

Ace RC
116 West 19th St.
Higginsville, MO 64037
Electronic kits, model kits, famous Silver Seven radios, Four Stroke Squadron.

Airtronics, Inc.
11 Autry
Irvine, CA 92718-2709
RC systems, kits.

Astro Flight
13311 Beach Ave.
Venice, CA 90291
Electric flight systems, kits.

B & B Specialties
14234 Cleveland Road
Granger, IN 46530
Quadra engines, Giant model supplies.

Balsa USA, Incorporated
201 Third Avenue
Menominee, MI 49858
Kits, including Giant Scale.

Bee Hive Model Aircraft
Box 744
Layton, UT 84041
Old-Timer kits.

Beemer RC West Distributors, Inc.
7725 E. Redfield Dr., Suite 105
Scottsdale, AZ 85260
Multiplex RC systems, sales and service.

Bell Rock Industries
6486 Hwy 179
Sedona, AZ 86336
Accessories, sanding tools.

Bob Martin RC Models
1520 Acoma Lander # C
Lake Havasu City, AZ 86403-2051
Sailplane kits.

Bob Violett Models
1373 Citrus Road
Winter Springs, FL 32708
Ducted fan kits, fan units, building supplies, composite construction materials.

Bridi Aircraft Designs, Inc.
23625 Pineforest Lane
Harbor City, CA 90710
Airplane kits, glow plugs, accessories.

Byron Originals
Box 279 Highway 59 and 175
Ida Grove, IA 51445
Giant Scale and ducted fan kits, engines, accessories.

C.B. Associates Incorporated
21658 Cloud Way
Hayward, CA 94545
Accessories, Giant Scale supplies.

Cannon RC Systems
2828 Cochran St.
Simi Valley, CA 93065
Lightweight miniature RC systems.

Carl Goldberg Models
4732 W. Chicago Ave.
Chicago, IL 60651
Trainer planes, scale kits, Jet adhesives, accessories.

Carlson Engine Imports
814 E. Marconi Avenue
Phoenix, AZ 85022
Imported engines: PAW, Aurora, Mills and Taplin reproductions, rare engines.

Champion Model Aero. Co.
P.O. Box 891
Woodbridge, NJ 07095
Airplane kits, including Old-Timers.

Chevron
P.O. Box 2480
Sandusky, OH 44870
Perfect brand paints.

Circus Hobbies
3132 South Highland Drive
Las Vegas, NV 89109
JR radio systems, kits, engines, accessories.

Cleveland Model and Supply
10309 Detroit Ave.
Cleveland, OH 44102
Hundreds of plans for scale and Old-Timer models, famous Cleveland kits.

Compuserve
5000 Arlington Centre Blvd.
Columbus, OH 43220
Personal computer network, includes ModelNet.

Condor Trading Company
27482 Capricho
Mission Viejo, CA 92692
Picco engines, electric motors, accessories.

Coverite
420 Babylon Road
Horsham, PA 19044
Covering materials, kits, accessories.

Cox Hobbies
1525 E. Warner
Santa Ana, CA 92705
.049 engines, kits, RC systems, ready-to-fly planes.

Craft Air Incorporated
20115 Nordhoff Street
Chatsworth, CA 91311
Kits, accessories.

Dave Brown Products
4560 Layhigh Road
Hamilton, OH 45013
Accessories, wheels, RC Flight Simulator for personal computers.

Dave Platt Models Inc.
6940 Northwest 45th St.
Plantation, FL 33313
Scale model kits.

Davey Systems Corp.
1 Wood Lane
Malvern, PA 19355
Sailplane kits, electric power kits, winches, electric motors, accessories.

Davis Diesel Development
Box 141
Milford, CT 06460
Conversion kits to Dieselize glow engines, accessories, fuel, tools.

Du-Bro Products
480 Bonner Road
Wauconda, IL 60084
Accessories, tools, wheels, hardware.

Dura Craft
1007 Orchard Grove Dr.
Royal Oak, MI 48067
Dura Plane trainer kits.

Dynathrust
2541 N. E. 11th Court
Pompano Beach, FL 33062
Propellers for large engines.

Edson Enterprises
17 Speer Place
Nutley, NJ 07110
Accessories, adjustable engine mounts.

Eldon J. Lind Company
Los Alamitos, CA 90720
Accessories, building boards, tools.

Eric Clutton—P.A.W. Diesels USA
913 Cedar Lane
Tullahoma, TN 37388-3167
Imported Diesel engines, fuel

FHS Supply
Rt. 5 Box 68
Clover, SC 29710
Red Max fuels, Diesel fuel, custom blends.

Flyline Models
10643 Ashby Place
Fairfax, VA 22030
Schoolyard Scale kits.

Fox Manufacturing
5305 Towson Ave.
Fort Smith, AR 72901
Model engines, spinners, glow plugs, tools, accessories.

Futaba
555 West Victoria
Compton, CA 90220
RC systems, accessories.

Gorham Model Products
23961 Craftsman Road
Calabasas, CA 91302
Helicopter kits, accessories, gyros.

Great Planes Manufacturing
706 West Bradley
Urbana, IL 61801
Model kits, accessories.

Grish Brothers
P.O. Box 248
St. John, IN 46373
Propellers, accessories.

H & N Electronics
10937 Rome Beauty Drive
California City, CA 93505
Electronic accessories, Supersafe solder flux.

Harry B. Higley & Sons, Incorporated
433 Arquilla Drive
Glenwood, IL 60425
Accessories, tools.

Hayes Products
1558 Osage Street
San Marcos, CA 92069
Tanks, motor mounts, accessories.

Herb's Model Motors
Box 61
Forksville, PA 18616
Antique reproduction engines and parts.

High Point Products
3013 Mary Kay Lane
Glenview, IL 60025
Prop balancing tools.

Hobby Horn
15173 Moran Street
Westminster, CA 92683
Old-Timer kits, electric kits, and flight systems.

Hobby Lobby International
Route 3 Franklin Pike Cir.
Brentwood, TN 37027
Craupner kits, accessories, tools, large catalog.

Hobby Shack
18480 Bandilier Circle
Fountain Valley, CA 92708
Kits, ready-to-fly planes, RC systems, engines, accessories; large catalog.

Indy RC
10620 N. College Ave.
Indianapolis, IN 46280
Kits, engines, ready-to-fly planes, large catalog.

J & Z Products
25029 South Vermont Avenue
Harbor City, CA 90710
Props, spinners, accessories.

JMD Fuel Labs
P.O. Box 235
North Olmstead, OH 44070
Custom blended fuels.

J'Tec
164 School St.
Daly City, CA 94014
Engine mounts, hardware, in-cowl mufflers, accessories.

Jet Hangar Hobbies
12554 Centralia Road
Lakewood, CA 90715
Ducted fan kits, fan power systems.

John Pond Old Time Plan Service
Box 3215
San Jose, CA 95156
Old-Timer plans.

Jomar
2028 Knightsbridge
Cincinnati, OH 45244
Electric motor speed controllers, engine sync systems, accessories.

K & B Manufacturing
12152 South Woodruff Avenue
Downey, CA 90241
Engines, fuels, epoxy paints, accessories.

Kraft Midwest
117 E. Main St.
Northville, MI 48167
RC system repair and tuning, Kraft radio parts.

Kress Technology
27 Mill Road
Lloyd Harbor, NY 11743
Tanks, accessories, ducted fan power systems.

Kustom Kraftsmanship
P.O. Box 2699
Laguna Hills, CA 92653
Accessories for .049 engines.

Lanier RC
Oakwood Road
Oakwood, GA 30566
Ready-to-fly airplane kits, accessories.

Larry Jolly Models
5501 West Como
Santa Ana, CA 92703
Sailplane and electric flight model kits.

Leisure Electronics
22971 B Triton Way
Laguna Hills, CA 92653
Electric flight systems, chargers, Old-Timer kits.

MRC
2500 Woodbridge
Edison, NJ 08817
Ready-to-fly airplanes, RC systems, radios, engines, model rockets, RC cars.

Mac's Products
8020 18th Avenue
Sacramento, CA 95826
Mufflers and tuned pipes for most model engines, accessories.

Major Decals
21 Fisher Avenue
E. Longmeadow, MA 01028
Decal and stick-on insignia sets and designs.

Mark's Models
1578 Osage
San Marcos, CA 92065
Fun scale kits, sailplane kits, accessories.

McDaniel RC Service
12421 Ransom Dr.
Glendale, MD 20769
Accessories, Ni-Starter glow plug batteries.

Micro Model Engineering
1301 West Lafayette
Sturgis, MI 49091
Reproduction parts for ignition engines.

Micro-X
P.O. Box 1063
Lorain, OH 44055
Kits, supplies, accessories.

Midwest Products
400 South Indiana
Hobart, IN 46342
Kits, accessories, wood and building supplies.

Miniature Aircraft Supply
2594 N. Orange Blossom Trail
Orlando, FL 32804
Helicopter kits, parts, and accessories.

Model Aviation Products
368 Tuckerton Road
Medford, NJ 08055
Mufflers, tuned pipes, accessories.

Model Engineering of Norwalk
54 Chestnut Hill
Norwalk, CT 06851
Kits, chargers, accessories.

Model Magic Products
P.O. Box 7784
St. Paul, MN 55119
Model Magic Filler, adhesives, fuel tubing, accessories.

Model Products Corp.
P.O. Box 314
Pompton Plains, NJ 07444
Head Lock glow plug connectors, D-Hinges, accessories.

Moody Tools
42-60 Crompton Avenue
East Greenwich, RI 02818
Precision miniature tool sets.

Morgan's Hobby Enterprises
200 West Lee St.
Enterprise, AL 36330
Cool Power fuel.

Nick Ziroli Models
29 Edgar Dr.
Smithtown, NY 11787
Giant Scale plans, accessories.

Norm Rosenstock Plans
94 Cedar Dr.
Plainview, NY 11803
Giant Scale plans.

Novak Electronics
2709 Orange Avenue, C
Santa Ana, CA 92707
RC receivers, speed controllers, electronic accessories.

Off the Ground Models, Inc.
606 C West Anthony Drive
Urbana, IL 61801
Sailplane kits.

Ohio Superstar Model Products
11376 Ridgeway Road
Kensington, OH 44427
Kits, accessories.

PIC Penn International Chemicals
943 Stierlin Road
Mountain View, CA 94043
Adhesives, chemical products.

PK Products
P.O. Box 6226
Hayward, CA 94540
Giant scale motors, accessories.

Pacer Technology
1600 Dell Ave.
Campbell, CA 95008
Adhesives.

Paul K. Guillow, Inc.
40 New Salem St.
Wakefield, MA 01880
Scale model kits.

Peck-Polymers
9962 Prospect, Suite L
Santee, CA 92071
Kits, supplies, RC blimp kit, CO_2 motors.

Pettit Paint Co. Inc.
36 Pine St.
Rockaway Boro, NJ 07866
Hobbypoxy adhesives and paints.

Pica Products
2657 N. E. 188th St.
Miami, FL 33180
Kits, adhesives, accessories.

Polk's Hobbies
346 Bergen Ave.
Jersey City, NJ 07304
Kits, engines, RC systems, accessories, tools.

Progress Manufacturing Company
P.O. Box 1306
Manhattan, KS 66502
Propellers.

RAM
4734 N. Milwaukee Ave.
Chicago, IL 60630
Electric accessories, speed controllers, boat kits.

RJL Industries
P.O. Box 5654
Pasadena, CA 91107
Engines, accessories, parts.

Repla-Tech International, Incorporated
48500 McKenzie Highway
Vida, OR 97488
Photos, plans, and documentation for scale aircraft.

Rhom Products Mfg. Corp.
908 65th St.
Brooklyn, NY 11219
Retractable landing gear, accessories.

Robart
310 North 5th
St. Charles, IL 60714
Tools, accessories.

Robbe Model Sport
180 Township Line Road
Bellemead, NJ 08502
Kits, almost-ready-to-fly airplanes, chargers, accessories.

Rocket City RC Specialties
103 Wholesale Ave., NE
Huntsville, AL 35811
Accessories, tools, hinges.

Roush Manufacturing
1728 Bywood St., SE
Canton, OH 44707-1224
Giant scale kits.

Royal Products Corporation
790 West Tennessee Ave.
Denver, CO 80223
Kits, ready-to-fly models, engines, accessories.

SR Batteries
P.O. Box 287
Bellport, NY 11713
High-performance batteries for RC systems, electric flight.

Satellite City
P.O. Box 836
Simi, CA 93062-0836
Hot Stuff CyA adhesives, accessories.

Scale Model Research
418 East Oceanfront
Newport Beach, CA 92661
Scale photos and documentation.

Scande Research, Incorporated
P.O. Box 133
Villa Park, IL 60181
Kits, accessories.

Shamrock Competition Imports
Box 26247
New Orleans, LA 70186
OPS engines, parts, accessories, glow plugs.

SIG Manufacturing
401 S. Front St.
Montezuma, IA 50171
Kits, engines, RC systems, paint and covering, accessories, large catalog.

Sonic-Tronics
7862 Mill Road
Elkins Park, PA 19117
Accessories, glow plugs, fuel pumps.

Standale Aircraft
2648 East Thornwood
Wyoming, MI 49509
Accessories.

Sterling Hobbies Inc.
3620 G St.
Philadelphia, PA 19134
Kits, RC and control line.

Sterner Engineering
661 Moorestown Drive
Bath, PA 18014
Ducted fan accessories and supplies.

Sullivan Products
1 N. Haven St.
Baltimore, MD 21224
Accessories, starters, pushrods, tanks, hardware.

Super Cyclone Engines
P.O. Box 10658
Phoenix, AZ 85064
Reproduction Old-Timer engines.

T & D Research Associates
6371 El Cajon Blvd.
San Diego, CA 92115
Edco Sky Devil replica engines, parts.

Tatone Products Corporation
1209 Geneva Avenue
San Francisco, CA 92412
Engine mounts, mufflers, accessories, test stands.

Technopower
610 North Street
Chagrin Falls, OH 44022
Radial four-stroke engines.

Top Flite Models
1901 N. Narragansett
Chicago, IL 60639
MonoKote covering, scale and sailplane kits, trainers, props.

Tower Hobbies
1608 Interstate Dr.
Champaign, IL 61821
Kits, engines, radio systems, large catalog.

U.S. Quadra
1032 East Manitowoc Avenue
Oakcreek, WI 53154
Quadra engines, props, accessories for giant scale.

Ultra Systems By Da Ca
6303 South 168th St.
Omaha, NE 68144
Field boxes, model support stands, accessories.

United Model Distributors
301 Holbrook Dr.
Wheeling, Il 60090
Engines, ready-to-fly planes.

W.E. Technical Services
P.O. Box 76884
Atlanta, GA 30328
Plans and drawings.

Williams Brothers Inc.
181 Pawnee St.
San Marcos, CA 92069
Parts and accessories for scale models, plastic kits, pilot figures.

Wilshire Model Center
2836 Santa Monica Boulevard
Santa Monica, CA 90404
Electric power systems, props, hard-to-find electric stuff.

Windsor Propeller Company
384 Tesconi Court
Santa Rosa, CA 95401
Master Airscrew props and accessories.

Wing Manufacturing
P.O. Box 33
Crystal Lake, IL 60014
Accessories, foam wing kits, model kits.

World Engines
8960 Rossash Ave.
Cincinnati, OH 45236
Engines, radio systems, ready-to-fly kits, accessories.

Yale Hobby Mfg.
20 Holly Lane
Wallingford, CT 06492
Helicopter blades, parts, and accessories.

Zenith Aviation Books
P.O. Box 1
Osceola, WI 54020
Reference books, magazines, videotapes, and calendars.

Zimpro Marketing
P.O. Box 3076
Oak Ridge, TN 37830
Ready-to-fly kits from Zimbabwe Model Products.

Appendix B

Magazines, Publishers, and Booksellers

Flying Models Magazine
Box 700
Newton, NJ 07860

Hannan's Runway
Box A
Escondido, CA 92025

Historic Aviation
3850 Coronation Road
Eagan, MN 55122

Kalmbach Publishing
1027 N. Seventh St.
Milwaukee, WI 53233

Midwest Technical Publications
1741 Big Bend
St. Louis, MO 63117

Model Airplane News
632 Danbury Road
Georgetown, CT 06829

Model Aviation Magazine
1810 Samuel Morse Drive
Reston, VA 22090

Model Builder Magazine
898 W. 16th St.
Newport Beach, CA 92663-2802

Model Shopper Magazine
524 Second St.
San Francisco, CA 94107

Motorbooks International
729 Prospect Ave.
Osceola, WI 54020

RC Report
P.O. Box 1706
Huntsville, AL 35807

RC Soaring Digest
P.O. Box 269
Peterborough, NH 03458

RC Video Magazine
Box 98
Lafayette, CO 80026

Radio Control Modeler Magazine
120 W. Sierra Madre Blvd.
Sierra Madre, CA 91023

Scale RC Modeler
7950 Deering Ave.
Canoga Park, CA 91304

Squadron/Signal Publications
1115 Crowley Drive
Carrollton, TX 75006

TAB Books
P.O. Box 40
Blue Ridge Summit, PA 17214

Appendix C

AMA Recognized Special Interest Groups

Officers' Name and Address	Sec/Treas.	Publication

Electric Aeromodeling Association

Robert A. Sliff, President
P.O. Box 9
Midway City, CA 92655

International Miniature Aircraft Association (IMAA)

		High Flight
Dick Phillips	Bill Wilbur	Les Hard
2070 Westbrook Drive	P.O. Box 501	2909 W. Mich. Ave.
Sidney, BC Canada V8L 4K1	Kittery, ME 03904	Lansing, MI 48917

International Miniature Aerobatic Club (IMAC)

		IMAC Newsletter
John Lockwood, President	C. Glenn Carter	C. Glenn Carter
1696 Griffith Avenue	2020 Gill Port Lane	
Clovis, CA 93612	Walnut Creek, CA 94598	

Miniature Aircraft Combat Association (MACA)

Phil Cartier, President
760 Waltonville RD.
Hummelstown, PA 17036
(312) 532-7349

Chris Gay
2018 Wessel Ct.
St. Charles, IL 60174
(312) 584-6015

MACA Newsletter
Dr. T.R. Passen
P.O. Box 111
Jasonville, IN 47438

National Association of Scale Aeromodelers (NASA)

John Guenther, President
R.R. 3, Box 261
Borden, IN 47106

Replica
Burt Dugan
11090 Phyllis Dr.
Clio, MI 48420

Navy Carrier Society (NCS)

Pete Mazur, President
5 W. Windsor Court
Aurora, IL 60504

Hi Low Landings
Melvin Schuette
P.O. Box 293
Auburn, KS 66402

National Free Flight Society (NFFS)

Tony Italiano, President
1655 Revere Drive
Brookfield, WI 53005

Free Flight Digest
Robert Meuser
707 Second St.
Davis, CA 95616

National Miniature Pylon Racing Association (NMPRA)

Henry Bartle, President
1353 N. Santiago
Santa Ana, CA 92701

Jill Bussell
4803 Fallon Place
Dallas, TX 75227

NMPRA
Karen Yeager
38238 Castle
Romulus, MI 48174

National Society of Radio Controlled Aerobatics (NSRCA)

Craig Millet, President
c/o Gibson, Dunn & Crutcher
P.O. Box 2490
Newport Beach, CA 92660

Suzi Stream
3723 Snowden Avenue
Long Beach, Ca 90808

K FACTOR
Betty Stream
3723 Snowden Avenue
Long Beach, CA 90808

National Soaring Society (NSS)

Peter Carr, President
229 Little Avenue
Ridgway, PA 15853

Dick Crowley
16413 E. Stanford Pl.
Aurora, CO 80015

Sailplane
Doug Dorton
3058 Bernina Drive
Salt Lake City, UT 84118

North American Speed Society

William Wisniewski
9222 Cedar Street
Canada V5C 5P7

Bev Wisniewski
9222 Cedar Street
Bellflower, CA 90706

Speed Times
Box 82294
North Burnaby, BC
Bellflower, CA 90706

Precision Aerobatics Model Pilots Association (PAMPA)

George Higgins
P.O. Box 561
N. Pembroke, MA 02358

Doug Figgs
329 Lincoln Place
Brooklyn, NY 11238

Pro Stunt News
Windy Urtnowski
9 Union Avenue
Littleferry, NJ 07643

Society of Antique Modelers (SAM)

Sal Taibi, President
4339 Conquista Ave.
Lakewood, CA 90713

Robert Dodds
2005 West Pine
Lodi, CA 95240

SAM Speaks
Jim Adams, Editor
2538 N. Spurgeon St.
Santa Ana, CA 92706

United Scale and Pattern Judges Association

Frank Broach, Sr.
463 S. Harrison Avenue
St. Louis, MO 63122

Russell Knetzger
2625 E. Shorewood Blvd.
Milwaukee, WI 53211

Appendix D

Academy of Model Aeronautics Insurance Facts

Accident/Medical Coverage

(Applies to individual members only)

This coverage works together with liability protection, but Accident/Medical applies to injury only, to reimburse an AMA member for medical expenses (also to reimburse the beneficiary for loss of life). Property damage is not involved. The Accident/Medical coverage applies to injuries resulting from model operation accidents regardless of who causes the accidents. AMA Liability Protection, however, applies to injury or property damage caused by an AMA member to someone else (see Comprehensive General Liability Coverage). The Accident/Medical coverage works as follows:

1. Provides up to $7,500 each for personal injury, and $1,500 for dismemberment or death.
2. Operates directly—does not require claim action by another person.
3. Pays upon submission of bills or other documents certifying cost of treatment.
4. Applies to model operation, in accordance with the AMA Safety Code.
5. Reimburses only for those expenses not covered by any other health plan.

What to do: If you are injured while engaged in the operation of models, please call the AMA to obtain a medical claim form and detailed instructions for filing your claim.

Fire, Vandalism, and Theft Coverage

(Applies to individual members only)

1. Provides up to $1,000 for loss of models and accessories, including RC equipment. Theft loss claims must be accompanied by a police report

and are evaluated in light of the information contained therein; i.e. whether stolen articles were, at the time of theft, in a locked or secured structure or conveyance and whether police found signs of forcible entry.

2. Except for first $100, which is deductible.
3. Coverage is "excess" to any other coverage which may be applicable.

Comprehensive General Liability Coverage

(Applies to individual members, clubs, chapters, and additional insureds)

1. For accidents arising from the operation of model aircraft, rockets, cars, and boats, in accordance with the AMA (or NAR) Safety Code.
2. Up to $1,000,000 per accident for bodily injury and/or property damage, subject to a $1,000,000 annual aggregate limit of liability which applies individually and collectively to all AMA members and additional insureds.
3. Covering all activities everywhere, whether competition or sport, provided that the original suit for damages is brought in the United States of America.
4. Involving member-to-member as well as member-to-nonmember accidents.
5. Coverage is "excess" to any other applicable coverage.
6. Except first $50 deductible (property damage only).
7. Any AMA member whose model causes an accident should report the accident and file a claim when liability is incurred.

Claim forms and step-by-step procedures for filing a claim are available from AMA HQ. In emergencies, contact HQ. Phone: (703) 435-0750. Ask for the Insurance Claim Representative in the Special Services Department.

Persons and Activities Insured under the AMA Insurance Coverage Provided to Chartered Club/Chapters and Members Thereof

A. The following PERSONS—as to their liability for activities of the club/chapter or for activities performed on behalf of the club/chapter, as follows:

1. Any chartered club/chapter officer (each of whom must be an AMA member), while acting within the scope of his position and in the performance of his duties.
2. Any active dues-paying chartered club/chapter member (who must also be an AMA member), as defined in the official club/chapter charter or bylaws.
3. Any owner of property used by the club (when named by the club as additional insured) for any official activities (meetings, flying sessions, car races, boating events, rocket shoots, contests, etc.) for which the club is liable.
4. Any honorary chartered club member, defined as one who is not a dues-paying club member and who does not participate regularly in club activities; such member must be listed on the charter application as honorary.
5. Any associate chartered club member is usually defined as wife, husband, child or parent of an active club member who does not operate models as part of the club's activity; such member must be listed on the charter application as an associate.

B. For the following ACTIVITIES—as to the liability of the club/chapter for activities scheduled or designated by club/chapter officers as official club/chapter events, such as:

1. Any meeting of the charter club/chapter, indoors or outdoors, involving modeling or nonmodeling activity, including club/chapter social and/or business affairs.
2. Any meet or contest sanctioned by the Academy of Model Aeronautics in which the club/chapter acts as sponsor and requires AMA membership of all contestants who participate by operating models.
3. Any model activity of the club/chapter provided that only AMA members are in-

volved in operating models (aircraft, cars, boats, or rockets).

4. Any club/chapter involving guests to the extent that the club's/chapter's liability is protected for the action of any guests, but non-AMA member guests themselves are not insured.

(Complete details of coverage(s) and exceptions are contained in master policies on file at AMA Headquarters, available for $1.00 per policy for handling and postage)

Appendix E

Academy of Model

Aeronautics Official Safety Code

General

1. I will not fly my model aircraft in competition or in the presence of spectators until it has been proven to be airworthy by having been previously, successfully flight tested.
2. I will not fly my model higher than approximately 400 feet within 3 miles of an airport without notifying the airport operator. I will give right-of-way to, and avoid flying in the proximity of full-scale aircraft. Where necessary, an observer shall be utilized to supervise flying to avoid having models fly in the proximity of full-scale aircraft.
3. Where established, I will abide by the safety rules for the flying site I use, and I will not willfully and deliberately fly my models in a careless, reckless, and/or dangerous manner.
4. If my model weighs over 20 pounds, I will only fly it in accordance with paragraph 5 of this section of the AMA Safety Code, with a minimum separation of 65 feet between spectators and flight operations.
5. At air shows or model flying demonstrations, a single straight line must be established, one side of which is for flying, with the other side for spectators. Only those persons essential to the flight operations are to be permitted on the flying side of the line; all others must be on the spectator side. Flying over the spectator side of the line is prohibited, unless beyond the control of the pilot(s).

   The only exceptions which may be permitted to the single straight line requirement under special circumstances involving consideration of site conditions and model size, weight, speed and power, must be jointly approved by the AMA President and the Executive Director. In any case, the maximum permissible weight of flying models is 55 pounds.

6. I will not fly my model unless it is identified with my name and address or AMA number on or in the model. NOTE: This does not apply to models flown indoors.

7. I will not operate models with metal-bladed propellers or with gaseous boosts, in which gases other than air at normal atmospheric pressure enter their internal combustion engine(s); nor will I operate models with extremely hazardous fuels; such as those containing tetranitromethane or hydrazine.

8. I will not operate models with pyrotechnics (any device that explodes, burns, or propels a projectile of any kind) including, but not limited to, rockets, explosive bombs dropped from models, smoke bombs, all explosive gases (such as hydrogen-filled balloons), ground mounted devices launching a projectile. The only exceptions permitted are rockets flown in accordance with the Safety Code of the National Association of Rocketry or those permanently attached (as per JATO use); also those items authorized for Air Show Team use as defined by the AST Advisory Committee (document available from AMA HQ).

NOTE: A model aircraft is defined as heavier-than-air craft with or without engine, not able to carry a human being.

Radio Control

1. I will have completed a successful radio equipment ground range check before the first flight of a new or repaired model.

2. I will not fly my model aircraft in the presence of spectators until I become a qualified flier, unless assisted by an experienced helper.

3. I will perform my initial turn after takeoff away from the pit, spectator, and parking areas, and I will not thereafter perform maneuvers, flights of any sort, or landing approaches over a pit, spectator, or parking area.

Free Flight

1. I will not launch my model aircraft unless at least 100 feet downwind of spectators and automobile parking.

2. I will not fly my model unless the launch area is clear of all persons except my mechanic and officials

3. I will employ the use of an adequate device in flight to extinguish any fuses on the model after it has completed its function.

Control Line

1. I will subject my complete control system (including safety thong, where applicable) to an inspection and pull test prior to flying.

2. I will assure that my flying area is safely clear of all utility wires or poles.

3. I will assure that my flying area is safely clear of all nonessential participants and spectators before permitting my engine to be started.

Appendix F
Academy of Model Aeronautics
Frequency Identification System
EFFECTIVE JANUARY 1988

PLAN NOW!

72 MHz AIRCRAFT USE ONLY

Single **RED** streamer—7/8" to 1" wide by 8" long affixed to the top of the transmitter antenna imprinted with above wording

1988-1991 AIRCRAFT FREQUENCIES

Channel No.	Frequency	Channel No.	Frequency	Channel No.	Frequency	Channel No.	Frequency
12	72.030	24	72.270	38	72.550	48	72.750
14	72.070	26	72.310	40	72.590	50	72.790
16	72.110	28	72.350	42	72.630	52	72.830
18	72.150	30	72.390	44	72.670	54	72.870
20	72.190	32	72.430	46	72.710	56	72.910
22	72.230	34	72.470				

Channels 12-34 Narrow Band transmitter only   Channel 36 and 58 not used—see General Info

CHANNEL NUMBER PLAQUES

One and one-half inch **BLACK** numerals with 1/4" stroke mounted on a white background, visible on both sides of the plaque.

At modeler's option, they may read horizontally or vertically and be attached at the base, center, or top of the antenna.

Non-reflective materials recommended.

GENERAL INFORMATION

Effective January 1988, channels 12 through 34 will be reserved for narrow-band transmitters only. Older, broad band equipment, as well as new narrow-band, can be operated on channels 38 through 56.

Channel 36 is not used in order to provide an 80 KHz spacing between channels 34 and 38.

Channel 58 is not used to provide image response protection for channel 12.

The channel usage and identification system is authorized for use in AMA sanctioned events and is highly recommended for all sport flying and club activities.

See pages 127-129 of the 1986-87 Official Model Aircraft Regulations for current frequency information and recommendations.

SEE OTHER SIDE FOR MORE INFORMATION

ACADEMY OF MODEL AERONAUTICS
1810 Samuel Morse Drive, Reston, VA 22090

12/86—RU

Academy of Model Aeronautics

FREQUENCY IDENTIFICATION SYSTEM
EFFECTIVE JANUARY 1988

PLAN NOW!

75 MHz SURFACE USE ONLY

Single **YELLOW** streamer—7/8" to 1" wide by 8" long affixed to the top of the transmitter antenna imprinted with above wording

1988-1991 SURFACE FREQUENCIES

Channel No.	Frequency	Channel No.	Frequency	Channel No.	Frequency
62	75.430	72	75.630	82	75.830
64	75.470	74	75.670	84	75.870
66	75.510	76	75.710	86	75.910
68	75.550	78	75.750	88	75.950
70	75.590	80	75.790	90	75.990

CHANNEL NUMBER PLAQUES

One and one-half inch **BLACK** numerals with 1/4" stroke mounted on a white background, visible on both sides of the plaque.

At modeler's option, they may read horizontally or vertically and be attached at the base, center, or top of the antenna.

Non-reflective materials recommended.

OTHER BANDS
(Model Aircraft **or** Surface Models)

27 MHz
Single, colored streamer or triangular flag—7/8" to 1" by 8"

26.995	Brown	27.095	Orange	27.195	Green
27.045	Red	27.145	Yellow	27.255	Blue

6 METER
Amateur Radio License Required

50 MHz
Single, **BLACK** streamer 7/8" to 1" by 8" and channel marker plaque

Channel No.	Frequency
00	50.800
02	50.840
04	50.880
06	50.920
08	50.960

53 MHz
Two colored streamers 7/8" to 1" wide by 8" long

Frequency	Colors	Frequency	Colors
53.100	Black-Brown	53.500	Black-Green
53.200	Black-Red	53.600	Black-Blue
53.300	Black-Orange	53.700	Black-Purple
53.400	Black-Yellow	53.800	Black-Gray

SEE OTHER SIDE FOR MORE INFORMATION

Appendix G

AMA District Frequency Coordinators

More information on radio interference problems can be obtained from these people. This list is current as of April 1987.

District 1: CT, ME, MA, NH, RI, VT
George Wilson
82 Frazier Way
Marston Mills, MA 02648

District 2: NY, NJ
George Myers
70 Froelich Farm Road
Hicksville, NY 11801

District 3: OH, PA, WV
James Bearden
5552 Foxrun Ct.
Cincinnati, OH 45239

District 4: DE, DC, MD, NC, VA
Paul Yacobucci
6408 Winthrop Dr.
Fayetteville, NC 28301

District 5: AL, FL, GA, MS, PR, SC, TN
Burnis Fields
P.O. Box 1063
Strickland Road
Interlachen, FL 32048

District 6: IL, IN, KY, MO
Loren Holm
3632 Main
Quincy, IL 62301

District 7: IA, MI, MN, WI
Bob Stamm
Box 357
Minoqua, WI 54548

District 8: AR, LA, NM, OK, TX
Scott Kalmus
814 West Centerville #125
Garland, TX 75041

District 9: CO, KS, NE, ND, SD, WY
Steve Mangles
Radio Service Center
918 S. Sheridan
Denver, CO 80226

District 10: AZ, CA, HI, NV, UT
George Steiner
2238 Rogue River Dr.
Sacramento, CA 95826

District 11: AK, ID, MT, OR, WA
Robert Balch
16439 S.E. Haig Dr.
Portland, OR 97236

Index

Index

Other Bestsellers From TAB

☐ **GUNSHIP: 82 CHALLENGING NEW ADVENTURES—Dave Prochnow**

Prepare for helicopter flight simulations so exciting and intense that the scenarios become missions, your computer becomes a cockpit, and you become a combat-sharp pilot. with this book and your Microprose Gunship software, you'll defend the U.S. in air battles of yesterday, today, and tomorrow. Four flight lessons give you the opportunity to practice keyboard "panel" operations, helicopter maneuvers, and Gunship program controls. 208 pp., 83 illus.
Paper $12.95   **Book No. 3032**

☐ **JET: 82 CHALLENGING NEW ADVENTURES —Dave Prochnow**

Exciting new scenarios for SubLOGIC'S bestselling jet flight simulator . . . including Korean and Vietnam War air battles! Here's your key to experiencing a whole new range of computer flying adventures with your JET flight simulator software . . . without having to buy expensive new scenery disks! For the IBM PC® or Commodore 64™/128™ user who wants to get the most excitement and authentic flight action from his JET software. 208 pp., 108 illus.
Paper $12.95   **Hard $19.95**
Book No. 2872

☐ **STRIP QUILTING—Diane Wold**

Diane Wold is an expert quilt-maker and her enthusiasm for the art of strip quilting is contagious. After introducing you to the tools, fabrics, techniques, and sewing methods used in strip quilting, she covers all the steps needed to complete a finished project including making borders, backing, using batting, basting, doing the actual quilting, and binding. You'll also find directions for using different types of patterns—multiple bands, one-band shifted patterns, and more. 184 pp., 165 illus. with 8 Full-Color Pages
Paper $12.95   **Hard $21.95**
Book No. 2822

☐ **WORKING WITH FIBERGLASS: Techniques and Projects—Jack Wiley**

With the expert instruction provided by this guide, you can use fiberglass to make model boats, flower pots, even garden furniture and hot tubs at a fraction of the commercially made price! These complete step-by-step instructions on laminating and molding make it simple to construct a wide variety of projects—including projects not available in manufactured versions. 226 pp., 252 illus.
Paper $11.95   **Hard $19.95**
Book No. 2739

☐ **YEAR-ROUND CRAFTS FOR KIDS —Barbara L. Dondiego, Illustrated by Jacqueline Cawley**

Easy to use, the handy month-by-month format provides a year of inspiring projects, many focused on seasonal themes to ensure young children's enthusiasm. Valentines, paper airplanes, and cookies for Easter, paper bag bunny puppets, string painting, Hanukkah candles and gingerbread boys, bell and candle mobiles and of course Christmas trees for December. And that's just the beginning. 256 pp., 180 illus., plus 8 pages of color
Paper $12.95   **Hard $19.95**
Book No. 2904

☐ **SHIP MODELING FROM STEM TO STERN —Milton Roth**

This guide is an individualized approach to ship model building. Emphasis is on a fuller understanding of the complexities of learning the skill and inspiring the model ship builder to strive for greater expertise. Written in an engaging, conversational style, the author is careful not to confuse or overburden you with technical terms. He painstakingly guides you through every aspect of model ship building. 288 pp., 324 illus., 4 full pages of color
Paper $17.95   **Book No. 2844**

☐ **REAL-LIFE SCENIC TECHNIQUES FOR MODEL RAILROADERS—Carl Caiati**

"Using commercially available equipment and components, (Caiati helps you) create customized equipment that can't be bought."

—Harold H. Carstens, Publisher, *Railroad Model Craftsman.*

If you're a model railroad enthusiast, this complete step-by-step guide is for you. It opens the door to creating elaborate pikes that are accurate to every last detail! 240 pp., 166 illus.
Paper $14.95   **Book No. 2765**

☐ **A MASTER CARVER'S LEGACY—essentials of wood carving techniques—Bouche'**

Expert guidance on the basics of wood carving from a master craftsman with over 50 years experience. All the techniques for making a whole range of woodcarved items are included. You'll learn how-to's for basic hip carving, the basic rose, cutting of twinings, a classic acanthus leaf, and a simple carving in the round. In no time at all you will be making many of the projects featured. 176 pp., 135 illus., 8½″ × 11″
Hard $24.95   **Book No. 2629**

Other Bestsellers From TAB

☐ **BOTTLING SHIPS AND HOUSES—Roush**

Written for the novice modeler and craftsman, this unique hobby guide is packed with ideas, tips, and techniques that even the advanced builder will find useful. It shows you, step-by-step, how to design and construct any type of house, building, ship, or boat inside a bottle. From choosing the right type of bottle, to adding the all-important finishing touches . . . the author has left nothing to chance. 224 pp., 208 illus., 16 pages in full color, 7″ × 10″
Paper $17.95   **Hard $22.95**
Book No. 1975

☐ **MAKING MONEY WITH YOUR MICROCOMPUTER —2nd Edition—Howard Parmington**

Let your PC pay for itself by putting it to work in your own profitable, part-time business. This newly revised, expanded, and updated idea book is overflowing with practical, proven business suggestions for getting started. Plus you'll find sources for software needed to get started. From setting up your office to locating the best market, all the factors that equal success are provided. 208 pp., 78 illus.
Paper $10.95   **Book No. 1969**

☐ **WORKING WITH ACRYLIC PLASTICS, INCLUDING 77 PROJECTS—Wiley**

Learn to make practical and attractive items out of plastic—an inexpensive and readily available material that is amazingly simple to work with. Now with these easy-to-follow instructions and show-how illustrations, you can learn to create all kinds of useful and decorative items from acrylic—home accessories, gifts, jewelry, art, furniture, dishes, and more! 256 pp., 328 illus., 7″ × 10″
Paper $11.95   **Book No. 1959**

☐ **ADVANCED AIRBRUSHING TECHNIQUES MADE SIMPLE—Caiati**

Here are all the professional tips and tricks needed to achieve the full spectrum of airbrushing effects—for retouching black-and-white and color photos, art and illustration work, mixed media, mural production, modeling and diorama finishing, vignetting and photo montage procedures, and more! Highlighted by more than 165 illustrations. 144 pp., 168 illus., plus 27 color plates, 7″ × 10″
Paper $14.95   **Book No. 1955**

☐ **DESIGNING AND CONSTRUCTING MOBILES—Wiley**

Discover the fun and satisfaction of learning to create exciting mobile art forms . . . to add a personal decorator touch to your home, as unique craft projects for a school class or club, even as a new income source! All the skills and techniques are here for the taking in this excellent, step-by-step guide to designing and constructing mobiles from paper, wood, metals, plastic, and other materials. 224 pp., 281 illus., 7″ × 10″.
Paper $12.95   **Hard $19.95**
Book No. 1839

☐ **CRAFTS FOR KIDS: A Month-By-Month Idea Book—Barbara L. Dondiego**

Creative and educational crafts for small children designed by a professional! More than 160 craft and cooking projects that can be made easily and inexpensively, from readily available materials! Step-by-step instructions plus exceptional illustrations enhance each project which are arranged by months to take advantage of special seasonal occasions! 224 pp., 156 illus.
Paper $10.95   **Hard $17.95**
Book No. 1784

*Prices subject to change without notice.

Look for these and other TAB books at your local bookstore.

TAB BOOKS Inc.
Blue Ridge Summit, PA 17294-0850

Send for FREE TAB Catalog describing over 1200 current titles in print.

OR CALL TOLL-FREE TODAY: **1-800-233-1128**
IN PENNSYLVANIA AND ALASKA, CALL: **717-794-2191**